The 9/11 Verses

Terrorist Teachings in the Koran

Karl J Trautwein

Now I See! Publishing

The 9/11 Verses
Terrorist Teachings in the Koran
by Karl J Trautwein

Published by:

Now I See! Publishing
P.O. Box 352
Etiwanda, CA 91739
Phone: 909-922-7276
Web site: www.The911Verses.com

Bible quotes taken from: Holy Bible: New International Version® (NIV®) Copyright© 1973, 1978, 1984 by International Bible Society.

Koran quotes taken from: The Koran: from the Original English Translation by J.M. Rodwell.

Hadith quotes titled "Muslim Hadith" are from the collection compiled by Adul Husain Muslim with English translation by Abdul Hamid Siddiqui.

Hadith quotes titled "Bukahari Hadith" are from the collection compiled by Abu Abdullah Muhammad with English translation by M. Muhsin Khan.

Library of Congress Control Number: 2008907281

ISBN: 978-0-9820273-0-1

Printed in the United States of America

0 9 8 7 6 5 4 3 2 1

Author Note:

The quotes and comments by the author are meant to inform — not to incite violence against people of any religious faith. God is love — those who show they hate by committing terrorist acts of violence, do not know God.

Dedication

For all those who have been deprived of life, liberty and the pursuit of happiness over the last 14 centuries.

Acknowledgments

First I want to thank all of you who have purchased *The 9/11 Verses*. You have shown that you have a desire to know the truth about terrorism and Islam. You understand that in order to remain a free society we need to be aware of threats to our freedom. The mainstream media intentionally misleads the public by withholding information on the terrorist teachings found in the Koran. *The 9/11 Verses* clearly proves that the Koran causes terrorism and makes us aware of the threat. Thanks for all your personal efforts to let others know about *The 9/11 Verses*. You have sent emails to your friends, family and associates. You have made phone calls and let people know about the book in conversations.

For her insights, ideas and support during the creative process I would like to thank my wife (she knows who she is). I would also like to thank the inventors of the Internet, whoever they may be. The information available on the World Wide Web provides a breadth and depth of knowledge that is only limited by ones ability to search creatively for it. The ability to look electronically for information saves many hours of research time.

There are many before me who have produced articles, books, blogs, personal stories and documentaries that place Islam under scrutiny. Collectively your work has served to stimulate my thoughts and has helped me develop my ideas for *The 9/11 Verses*.

Carolyn Porter and Alan Gadney of One-on-One Book Production and Marketing have been extremely supportive with suggestions that have made this book better. They have also helped keep me on the straight and narrow as to the rules of the English language and clear communication. It has been great to be able work together with them and draw from their wisdom.

Freedom is such an amazing blessing. To have access to information and be able to form your own conclusions is surely a God given right. Thanks to all those who have established our political system and helped to protect our freedom. In America, no faith, philosophy or system of thought is above critical examination and scrutiny.

Karl J. Trautwein
September 2008

Contents

بِسْمِ اللهِ الرَّحْمٰنِ الرَّحِيْمِ

The 9/11 Verses

What Are We to Think About the Muslim Faith?

> *Love your neighbor as yourself*
> **Jesus Christ**

> *Believers! Wage war against such of the infidels as are your neighbors*
> **Allah**

This book is the end of a journey. It is a journey that will be easier and shorter for you than it was for me, as I have gathered all the information for your consideration in one place. This journey began for me on September 11, 2001. It began with a simple question. What am I to think about the Muslim faith?

In the past I had no objection to Muslims and their faith. Like most Americans in a primarily "Christian" country I really knew little about Muslims or their beliefs. However, I thought I saw some things that my Christian faith had in common with Islam.

For one thing we both believe that there is one true God who created all there is. We also share a common moral code that follows most of the Ten Commandments and seeks to live a life that is pleasing to our creator. Both faiths believe in a day of judgment when God will examine our lives. Likewise, the two

1

faiths teach that after death we will continue to live on eternally, either with God, or apart from Him.

Even though I believe my faith in Christ to be true, like most Christians in the United States and around the world, I had no ill will towards others worshiping freely as they believe. I freely came to my belief in Christ. How could I not support freedom of conscience for others when it comes to matters of faith? So in the past I had no strong negative feelings towards Islam.

September 11th, 2001

On the morning of September 11, 2001, I remember watching the burning towers, in stunned disbelief, just before commuting to my office in Riverside, California. Driving southbound on the 15 freeway, I listened to Bill Handle on KFI AM 640 as he tried to piece together what was happening. It was chaos.

Productivity at the office fell as we all compared notes about the latest information on the attacks. Many of my co-workers were in shock. Some of them organized a prayer meeting. Prayers were said. Tears were shed. One of my business associates had been at a lunch meeting on the top of one of the towers just that year. There was tension and fear in the air. Was this what it was like when Pearl Harbor was attacked in December 1941?

My next few nights were consumed with watching various news reports on the attacks. Activities other than work came to a standstill. I live in Southern California east of Los Angeles. A relaxing evening would find me reading a good book while enjoying a warm California night on the balcony off our master bedroom. The balcony faces south with an unobstructed view of the flight paths to Ontario and Los Angeles International airports.

I once read that 25 percent of the air traffic in the entire country is in the skies of Southern California. That being the case, if you were on my balcony and looked into the sky, you would see several planes in the air lined up in rows along flight paths for landings at the two airports. At night their headlights looked like slow moving falling stars.

After 9/11 the sky was empty. The Bush administration suspended all air traffic for three days. Never before had there been a night without "slow falling stars" in the sky over Southern California. It was an apocalyptic like feeling to view the empty night sky.

At the twin towers site, cable news showed scores of medical personal waiting at casualty receiving centers for patients that never came. Hundreds of family members stood with pictures of their missing loved ones searching in vain, hoping that they were alive. As time went on recordings and stories of phone calls made by people caught up in the attack came out in news reports and on the Internet. There were calls made from doomed planes in the air and calls from those trapped in the burning towers.

Some of the victims were angry, some were scared, some said their good-byes with prayers, love and thoughts of those they were going to leave behind. I listened to one recorded call between a 911 operator and a man trapped in one of the burning towers. He told the operator he was too young to die. He and his co-workers had young children at home who needed them. As he finished saying this, you could hear an awful roar as the building above collapsed. The man's last words screamed out were "Oh God! Oh…" as he was crushed to death. This was horrible and real.

Is murder and violence a part of Islam?

The attacks of September 11, 2001 changed everything. I began a journey to understand Islam. I wanted to find out for me and countless others if the acts of murder committed by Muslims that day and before were a part of Islam or not. Were the 9/11 perpetrators extremist in their views and in their interpretation of their faith? Did they misread their scriptures? Did their actions have anything at all to do with Islam?

The 9/11 Verses

Society is full of political correctness when it comes to non-Christian faiths. So the news reporting was not giving me much help in finding any answers. All I kept hearing was that terrorist attacks were not "true Islam." That "true Islam" is a "religion of peace." Other commentators would say that terrorist attacks are political or economic but not religious in nature.

Yet, no one gave any proof for their assertions. I never heard or saw any analysis of what Islam teaches about terrorism. What are Muslims taught about people outside Islam? Does Islam teach anything about violence and killing? How are Muslims taught to treat non-Muslims? Does the Koran really teach that if you blow yourself up in a suicide mission that you go straight to heaven and enjoy 72 virgins? Why are almost all terrorist acts committed by those who claim to be Muslim? These and my many other questions plagued me and started me on my journey for answers.

I start to ask questions about Islam

September 11th caused me to question and want to understand Islam. How could 19 Muslims murder 3000 people and call it service to God? Why were there few or no Muslims in the world rising up to condemn what had been done in the name of their God? To the contrary, I watched video with thousands of Muslims dancing in the streets of Lebanon, the West Bank and Gaza with joy over the attacks.

The 9/11 hijackers left taped last wills that were released after the attack. In them are quotes of Muslim scriptures. The terrorists call all Muslims to the duty of holy war. They speak of what they are doing as pleasing to Allah.

In the years following the attack more brutal acts were done in the name of Allah. As I found out when researching this book, Muslims murdering people for Allah had been going on for ages — long before 9/11.

4

Thousands of violent attacks by Muslims

In fact there have been thousands of attacks by Muslims over just the last 50 years alone. Many people like you and I have been murdered while just going about their daily lives. Muslim attackers have killed with guns, knives and explosives. Many of the attacks have been purposely planned so that the attacker himself is killed (martyred) in the assault. According to the website www.thereligionofpeace.com, as of May 2008, Muslims have carried out 11,098 attacks since 9/11. Here are a few examples.

- In October 2001 Muslims attacked a Christian church in Pakistan killing 17 worshipers.

- *Wall Street Journal* reporter Daniel Pearl was kidnapped in Pakistan on January 23rd, 2002. A video showed Muslims forcing him to make a statement about his and his families Jewish background. Then the Muslim kidnappers slowly cut off his head. Pearl's body was cut into 10 pieces and buried in a shallow grave.

- Muslims threw grenades into the Protestant Inter-national Church in Pakistan in March 2002, killing five innocent people.

- On August 6, 2003, a Muslim Saudi college student cut the throat of a Jewish student with a four-inch knife in Houston, Texas.

- A pregnant women and four children were murdered in Gaza on 05/02/2004 by Muslims who were members of a group called "Party of Allah."

- On 05/11/2004 civilian Nick Berg had his head sawed off by Muslims in Iraq as they chanted to cover up his screams.

The 9/11 Verses

- Muslims sawed off the head of Kim Sun-il, a Korean Christian, in Iraq on 06/22/2004.

- Muslims exploded bombs in London killing 52 on 07/07/05.

- In June of 06 a Muslim shot four co-workers and a police officer in Denver, Colorado saying it was "Allah's choice."

- In Seattle, Washington on 07/28/06, a Muslim shot six women at a Jewish center.

- In April 2007 five Muslims tied up three Christian men in Istanbul, Turkey and slit their throats.

On February 3, 2006, London was the site of angry protests by Muslims over Scandinavian publications of cartoons of the prophet Muhammad. Pictures show Muslims with signs that read, **"slay those who insult Islam," "Europe you will pay demolition is on the way," "behead those who insult Islam," "butcher those who mock Islam," "Europe you will pay — your extermination is on the way," "Europe is the cancer, Islam is the answer," "exterminate those who slander Islam," "Europe you will pay — your 9/11 is on it's way,"** My personal favorite was, **"Freedom go to hell."**

These slogans are not just words. The violence depicted on those signs had actually been done by Muslims during our lifetimes.

As I have watched or read these stories over the last several years, I have continued to question why Muslims are committing so much violence. President Bush, other politicians, and a few Muslim leaders have said that Islam is a religion of peace. According to them, violence against innocent people is not a part of true Islam. Thousands of violent acts have happened because a small minority of Muslims have "hijacked" the Islamic faith.

These so-called "hijackers" have twisted Islamic teachings and used them as a justification to kill and murder in the name of Allah.

Others have claimed that Islam has inherent violence in its doctrines and beliefs, which is why there are thousands of violent attacks by Muslims. So who is right?

I find it odd that Islam calls themselves a "religion of peace." There are no other faiths that I have ever heard called a "religion of peace." Is it that Muslims commit so much violence in the name of Islam that the term "religion of peace" had to be invented?

Muslims have committed thousands of acts of killing and violence before and after September 11th. Yet for some reason September 11th seems to be a defining point for many people. I suppose this is because of the grand scale of killing and destruction that the attacks produced in our United States. It captures the imagination and causes one to search for answers to understand that terrible event.

9/11 has caused Muslims to question their faith

Strangely enough, the fall of the twin towers has become a defining point for many Muslims to question their faith and leave Islam. You can read their stories on the Internet. Some Muslims are saying if Osama Bin Laden and other terrorist leaders are spiritual leaders in Islam as well, then there has got to be some flaw in the religion.

Other Muslims have left the faith because they have read the Islamic scriptures for themselves and have been shocked at the level of hate and violence within the pages. Most Muslims are decent human beings. They do not want to live in a constant state of emotional hatred toward those who do not believe in Islam.

I would guess that the majority of followers of any faith have not completely read and studied in depth their own scriptures. So there are Muslims that are not familiar with the passages that we will be reviewing in this book. But knowing these teachings of Islam does shed light on how the Muslim terrorists think.

I read the Holy Writings of Islam

After 9/11, I decided to find out the truth about Islam. I did not want to listen to second or third hand information about the faith. I wanted to find out for myself. So I have read the Holy Writings of Islam which are the Koran and the Hadith.

The Koran is the message that Allah gave to Muhammad. Like the Bible, the words of the Koran are said to be the very words of God. The Hadith contains narrated writings about the life of Muhammad. These writings show what Muhammad said, what he did, what he approved and disapproved. Muhammad's sayings and actions are considered by Muslims to be Allah's divine law equal to the Koran.

Faithful Muslims use these Holy Writings to tell them how to practice their faith. After personally reading the Koran and Hadith, I now understand why the 11,098 violent acts were committed by Muslims since 9/11.

What would Muhammad do?

Maybe you have heard a saying that Christians have used in recent years, "what would Jesus do." I have seen this on bumper stickers and wrist bracelets, "WWJD." My wife was in the parking lot of a store the other day and observed a man on his cell phone using a string of curse words that would have made the profanity gods very happy. On the back of the man's car was a bumper sticker that said, "WWSD – what would Satan do." You might be thinking, "only in California." You are probably right!

Some Christians, when thinking about how to treat others or how to handle a situation, try to determine what Jesus would do if in the same situation. Christians learn about Jesus from reading the Bible, which tells us what Jesus said and did.

In the same way Muslim followers look at what Muhammad said and did as shown in the Hadith to decide how to live and act. In a sense they ask themselves the question, what would Muhammad do (WWMD).

My religious point of reference is Christianity. As I took my journey through Islam, I found myself automatically comparing Muhammad's teachings to those of my faith. Not all citizens in the United States and the western world are Christians. However society in the United States and the western world is a product of Christian thought and principles.

Society in the Islamic World is a product of Islamic thought and principles. Christian thought and Islamic thought are very different. In order to illustrate these differences, I have made many comparisons between Christian and Islamic Scriptures.

The verses I present in the following chapters will be for the most part the ones that advocate violence against non-Muslims. It does not seem to me to matter that the Koran contains verses that advocate peace with non-Muslims. Just the fact that the Islamic scriptures have passages that call for hate and violence is enough to fuel acts of murder against people today. As you will see when you combine the Koran with the sayings and actions of Muhammad the motivation for violence is strong.

The 9/11 Verses

I have called this book *The 9/11 Verses* for two main reasons. 9/11 was the cause of my desire to discover if Islam is about peace or violence. Without 9/11, I would have never even asked the question.

My second reason is that 9/11 now stands as the ultimate example of terrorist violence. This was violence and murder on a grand scale. Correspondingly the teachings of Islam have inspired violence and murder on a monumental scale.

Although the Islamic Holy Writings are readily available, I speak of these teachings as "hidden" and "secret." This is because they have been largely kept out of the public debate about violence and Islam. The Koran verses and Hadith passages I unveil in this book have, in effect, been kept a secret and hidden from public view. I know this because although I am well read, and follow news stories closely, I have never before seen or heard the Islamic texts in this book, in the mainstream media.

Yet these very verses and passages are why we see so much violence by Muslims. I will show you how these texts work together to cause Muslims to commit violent terrorist acts. You will not need a secret code to uncover the meaning of these texts. The passages are straightforward and easy to understand. As you read them, I believe that you also will come to think of them as *The 9/11 Verses*.

بِسْمِ اللهِ الرَّحْمٰنِ الرَّحِيْمِ

Islam 101

You have heard that it was said,
"Love your neighbor and hate your enemy."
But I tell you love your enemies and
pray for those who persecute you.

Jesus Christ

When ye encounter the infidels, strike off their heads
till ye have made a great slaughter among them.

Allah

efore I show you *The 9/11 Verses*, there are a few things you need to know and understand about Islam. I will not be covering everything about the faith. My purpose here is to go over some of the fundamentals of Islam that are needed to understand our subject.

I begin with the meaning of the words "Islam" and "Muslim." Islam is an Arabic word which means total surrender and submission to Allah. A Muslim is someone who has surrendered and submitted to Allah.

Another word that appears hundreds of times in Islamic writings is "Infidel." The actual Arab word for "Infidels" is Kafiroon. Kafiroon literally means "those who reject." So an infidel is anyone who rejects the message of Islam. Therefore all non-Muslims are infidels. Do not confuse this with "Apostate." An apostate is someone who at one time professed to be a Muslim but has left the faith.

The 9/11 Verses

The Islamic Holy Writings were originally written in Arabic. When translating names from one language to another, an attempt is made to get the sound of the name to be the same in the new language as the original. In some cases there are no equivalent sounds made by letters in English for words in Arabic. That is why the primary Islamic Holy Book is spelled in English both Koran and Qur'an. There are also variations on the English spelling of the name Muhammad. I have elected to use "Koran" and "Muhammad" throughout this book.

There are said to be about 1.3 billion Muslims in the world today. This is about 21 percent of the current world population. Christians, at 2.1 billion, are estimated to be 33 percent of the world population.

Islam is a monotheistic faith and absolute in its belief that there is only one true God. The name of this true God is Allah. "Allah" is an Arabic word that probably comes from the word "al-ilah" which means "the deity." According to the Koran one of the worst sins you can commit is to add any other gods to Allah. Allah has no partners or associates. Any faith that believes in many gods is committing this sin.

Christians, in the eyes of Muslims, commit this sin by believing in the Trinity. The doctrine of the Trinity teaches that God is three in one. The Father, the Son (Jesus), and the Holy Spirit are all God. The Koran is clear that Allah has no associates or partners. If you add gods to Allah you will burn in hell.

Infidels now are they who say, "God is the Messiah, son of Mary;" for the Messiah said, "O children of Israel! Worship God, my Lord and your Lord." Whoever shall join other gods with Allah, Allah shall forbid him the Garden, and his abode shall be the Fire; and the wicked shall have no helpers. They

surely are infidels who say, "God is the third of three:" for there is no God but one God: and if they refrain not from what they say, a grievous chastisement shall light on such of them as are infidels. **The Koran, Chapter 5:76-77**

Anyone who is a Christian believes that Jesus is God. Christ is called "Immanuel" which means "God with us." Paul writes that Christ is equal to God and came down from heaven becoming a man. Jesus himself in the gospels on numerous occasions said and did things that showed he was claiming to be equal to God. Therefore all 2.1 billion Christians according to the Koran are not allowed to go to the "Garden" (heaven) and instead will be in the "fire" (hell).

Islam teaches that Allah is the same God that the Jewish and Christian faiths worship. Muslims claim that the English translation of Allah would be "God." What they really mean is that the one true God is Allah. Muslims do not believe that the Jewish and Christians doctrines about God are true. So from the Jewish and Christian perspective, Allah is not the same deity as the Jewish and Christian God. Therefore in this book I have used the name "Allah" for any Islamic reference to their God.

The Holy Writings of Islam

The Koran is the message of Allah given to Muhammad by the angel Gabriel. The Hadith are the words and deeds of Muhammad written down after his death. The Arabic word Hadith means "sayings." The Hadith shows the way Muhammad lived his life and of what he approved and disapproved. These writings taken together are the "Holy Writings" of Islam.

The word "Koran" literally means "the recitation." The recitations in the Koran are called "verses." The meaning of "verses" is that they are "signs." That is the verses are signs or messages from Allah to point you to the true faith which is Islam.

The 9/11 Verses

There are hundreds of thousands of hadith. Some hadith are considered reliable while others are not. I have chosen to use the hadith collections compiled by Muslim and Bukhari as sources for this book. Muslim and Bukhari expended much effort to ensure the authenticity of their collections. Each hadith was checked for its compatibility with the Koran. Also, the reliability and truthfulness of those who reported what Muhammad said was checked. Muslim reviewed 300,000 hadith and included only 4,000 based on his stringent acceptance criteria. Bukhari worked for 16 years to end up with 2,602 hadith. The Muslim and Bukhari hadith collections are recognized by the Muslim world as among the most authentic.

Finding the historical truth about how the Holy Writings of Islam were compiled is difficult. Here are some selected opinions from my review of various writers on the subject.

Muhammad recited the verses from Gabriel but did not write them down. His followers put them on paper and compiled them into a holy book, the Koran. For hundreds of years after Muhammad died there were various versions in circulation. At some point the Koran was standardized into the form we have today. Likewise, the things that the prophet said and did, the Hadith, were not written down by him. Muhammad's followers wrote down his actions and sayings in narrative form, and compiled them together.

It is impossible to know if the Holy Writings we have today are exactly what Muhammad said and did. In the Hadith one of Muhammad's wives and other early followers are quoted as saying there are missing and altered verses in the Koran.

However, Islam teaches that the Holy Writings are accurate. The Koran is taken by faith to be the true words of Allah relayed by Gabriel, the messenger of God, to the prophet Muhammad. The Hadith is likewise taken by faith to be what Muhammad truly said and did.

Muhammad is the Muslim Faith

The prophet Muhammad is the central person to the faith. Just as Christ was the founder of Christianity, Muhammad was the founder of Islam. Muhammad lived in Mecca, which is in today's Saudi Arabia, about 1400 years ago. So the Christian faith was already 600 years old when he came along.

Muhammad would, from time to time, go into the hills by Mecca for a retreat of religious contemplation. He would sit in a cave spending time in meditation and religious thought.

While on one of his retreats, at the age of 40, Muhammad in 610 AD, began to receive a series of revelations from the angel Gabriel. Gabriel appears in the Bible four times. Gabriel is an archangel, which means he is one of the top high-ranking angels. His name means, "power of God." In the Bible, Gabriel is most famous for being the angel that announced to Mary that she would give birth to Jesus.

Muhammad's revelations continued over a period of 22 years during which he memorized and recited them to his followers. The Koran calls Muhammad a "noble pattern" worthy of imitation. Muslims are called to be imitators of the prophet in how they live their lives. This is the same concept that Christianity teaches about its founder. Christians are called to be imitators of Christ.

The Five pillars of Islam

Being "Muslim" means that you have surrendered to Allah and submitted to His will. To submit to Allah a follower is required to perform the five pillars of the faith. These are declaring your faith, prayer, Ramadan fasting, giving to the needy, and making a pilgrimage to Mecca. Here is a brief explanation of each of the five pillars of Islam.

The 9/11 Verses

Pillar One – Declaring your faith

The declaration of faith is simple. You just say out loud "There is no god but Allah, and Muhammad is the messenger of Allah."

Pillar Two – Prayer

Prayers are to be performed five times per day at dawn, noon, mid-afternoon, sunset and nightfall. The prayers are set recitations that contain verses from the Koran. They are said in Arabic. Personal prayers may also be said in your own language. The worshiper must be ritually clean and the place of prayer must be clean. As you pray you must be facing the "Kaaba" which is in Mecca.

Pillar Three – Giving to the needy

Giving to the needy is called the "Zakat." This involves an Islamic formula for donations to the poor. There are different rates and applications of the formula, but in simple terms, it works out to about two-point-five percent of the wealth you have left over after meeting the needs of your family. Muslims pay the Zakat each year.

Pillar Four – Fasting during the month of Ramadan

During the month of Ramadan, from the first light until sundown, a Muslim is required to not eat or drink or have sexual relations. Ramadan is Holy because it is the month that the revelations from the angel Gabriel began. There are exemptions given for children, and those who are sick, old or otherwise not able to fast.

Pillar Five – Pilgrimage to Mecca

Muslims who are healthy enough and have the finances to do so, must make a pilgrimage to Mecca. This is required at least once in a Muslim's lifetime. The Kaaba is the most holy site of Islam and is in Mecca. The Kaaba

16

is a structure that Muslims believe Abraham built as a house of monotheistic worship.

This pilgrimage is called the "Hajj." There are various places the pilgrim is required to visit in Mecca and several rituals that are required to be performed.

Muhammad gave the last message from God

Muslims believe that Muhammad has given the final and last message from God. They believe the message is the same one that all other messengers from God such as Abraham, Moses and Christ preached. According to Islam, Muhammad did not start a new faith but restored the lost true faith.

Judaism and Christianity are corruptions of the one true faith—Islam

The Koran teaches that the message Allah gave to Muhammad is the same one that God has in the past given to various Prophets, the Jewish people, and the one that Jesus preached.

Say ye: "We believe in Allah, and that which hath been sent down to us, and that which hath been sent down to Abraham and Ismael and Isaac and Jacob and the tribes: and that which hath been given to Moses and to Jesus, and that which was given to the prophets from their Lord. No difference do we make between any of them…" **The Koran, Chapter 2:130**

Wherever the Holy Writings of Christians or Jews conflict with the Holy writings of Islam, the former are said to be corrupted. For example Christ in the Bible says he is equal to God and the Bible teaches He is God. The Koran says that Christ was just a man, not God. So the Bible is corrupt.

According to Islam, if the words in the Bible had not been corrupted, the Jewish prophets, Jesus, and the New Testament authors would have a message identical to that of the Koran. In fact the Koran says that Abraham and Christ are prophets and were Muslims.

The Holy Writings of Islam show Muslims how they should live their lives

The Holy Writings are very detailed and cover almost all areas of life. The Hadith and Koran contain page after page of directions on how to live.

For example women are not to be out in public without a male relative. Laws of inheritance say that males must be given two times the share of females. Muhammad requires that women are to be covered from head to toe when out in public. Other laws cover what to eat and not eat with all pork strictly forbidden. Any drinking of alcohol is not allowed.

I remember a story out of Iraq that a Muslim shot a Christian store owner to death for selling beer even though non-Muslims were given the freedom to do so by the lawmakers in Iraq. I have no problem with a faith having rules and laws. Orthodox Jews have many similar laws in their faith. The problem comes when a faith calls its followers to force others, who do not believe, to obey its rules and laws.

In an Islamic State, Muslim lawmakers translate Allah's will into laws that people in their society are required to obey. Saudi Arabia is one of the strictest Muslim countries.

Recently, a 19-year-old girl went out in public without a male relative. She was attacked and gang raped. The police arrested her, and she was convicted of the crime of being in public without a male relative. Her sentence was 200 lashes with a whip. This is in keeping with Muhammad's command that women are not to be out in public without a male relative.

Islam's Holy Writings contain the seeds of violence

As I read through the Holy Writings of Islam, I noticed that there were verses calling for justice, mercy and kindness. These passages were not unlike those found in the Bible of my Christian faith. However, I was stunned by the Islamic verses calling for violence against non-Muslims.

As a prime example, read the quotes from Jesus and Allah at the beginning of this chapter. As a Christian I was always taught to love my neighbor as myself. My neighbor is anyone who is in need. An example of this in the Bible, is the story of the Good Samaritan told by Jesus.

Jews in the time of Jesus did not associate with Samaritans. Samaritans were outcasts that were looked down upon and seen as worthless. This story shows what a Christian's attitude should be towards others who are in need no matter who they are.

✠

The story of the Good Samaritan

On one occasion an expert in the law stood up to test Jesus. "Teacher," he asked, "what must I do to inherit eternal life?" "What is written in the Law?" he replied. "How do you read it?" He answered: "Love the Lord your God with all your heart and with all your soul and with all your mind;" and, "Love your neighbor as yourself." "You have answered correctly," Jesus replied. "Do this and you will live." But he wanted to justify himself, so he asked Jesus, "And who is my neighbor?"

The 9/11 Verses

In reply Jesus said: "A man was going down from Jerusalem to Jericho, when he fell into the hands of robbers. They stripped him of all his clothes, and went away, leaving him half-dead. A priest happened to be going down the same road, and when he saw the man, he passed by on the other side. So too, a Levite, when he came to the place and saw him, passed by on the other side.

But a Samaritan, as he traveled, came where the man was; and when he saw him he took pity on him. He went to him and bandaged his wounds, pouring on oil and wine. Then he put the man on his own donkey, took him to an inn and took care of him. The next day he took out two silver coins and gave them to the innkeeper.

"Look after him," he said, "and when I return, I will reimburse you for any extra expense you may have." Which of these three do you think was a neighbor to the man who fell into the hands of robbers? The expert in the Law replied, "The one who had mercy on him."

Luke 10:25-37

The point Jesus was making in the story is that God wants us to love our neighbor. A neighbor is not defined by color, race, gender or religion. A neighbor is anyone in need. The so-called "religious" people, the Jewish priest and Jewish Levite (an assistant to the temple priests), did not get it. The outcast Samaritan man who had the "wrong" faith got it right. Faith that pleases God is not only about beliefs and rules to follow. God is concerned about how we treat others.

Allah and Muhammad give commands to kill, maim, decapitate and imprison non-Muslims. These *9/11 Verses* sow the seeds of violence in Islam.

Islamic Holy Writings teach tolerance and peace but they also teach hate and violence

When I read the Islamic Holy Writings, I noticed that there are many passages that contradict themselves by commanding opposite actions. Take the subject of wine and gambling, for instance. The Koran, Chapter 2:219, says that wine and games of chance has some advantage for men. While in Chapter 5:91, the Koran declares that wine and gambling are an abomination of Satan's work. How can "Satan's work" be advantageous for man? The first verse seems to say it is ok to drink wine while the second declares wine to be off limits.

The Koran and Hadith contain many commands that contradict other commands. As I discussed before, some passages direct Muslims to be kind, merciful and tolerant of non-Muslims. Those who say Islam is a religion of peace quote these verses to prove their claims. Then, there are other verses that command killing and violence against non-Muslims. In order to compare the contradictory messages here are some examples.

�֍ **Peaceful**

> *Let there be no compulsion in religion...*
> **The Koran, Chapter 2:257**

�֍ **Violent**

> *...kill those who join other gods with Allah (polytheist Arabs) wherever ye shall find them; and seize them; besiege them, and lay wait for them with every kind of ambush: but if they shall convert, and observe prayer, and pay the obligatory alms, then let them go their way, for Allah is gracious, merciful.* **The Koran, Chapter 9:4**

Peaceful

They who believe (Muslims), and they who follow the Jewish religion, and the Christians... shall have their reward with their Lord. The Koran, Chapter 2:59

Violent

Muslim Hadith book 019 Number 4366

"I (Muhammad) will expel the Jews and Christians from the Arabian Peninsula and will not leave any but Muslim"

Tolerant

Who gives alms (money to the poor), alike in prosperity and in success, and who master their anger, and forgive others! Allah loveth the doers of good.

The Koran, Chapter 3:128

O my son! Observe prayer, and enjoin the right and forbid the wrong, and be patient under whatever shall betide thee: for this is a bounden duty.

The Koran, Chapter 31:16

Intolerant

O believers! take not the Jews or Christians as friends. They are but one another's friends. If any one of you taketh them for his friends, he surely is one of them! Allah will not guide the evil doers.

The Koran, Chapter 5:56

That of His bounty He may reward those who have believed and wrought righteousness, for the unbelievers He (Allah) loveth not.

The Koran, Chapter 30:44

Muhammad is the Apostle of Allah; and his comrades are vehement against the infidels, but full of tenderness among themselves...

The Koran, Chapter 48:29

Which of these commands are good faithful Muslims supposed to obey? The Koran itself tells us how to fix the problem of verses commanding opposite actions.

When verses contradict each other, the earlier commands are cancelled and overridden by the later verses.

Whatever verses we cancel, or cause thee to forget, We bring a better or its like. Knowest thou not that Allah has power over all things?

The Koran, Chapter 2:100

This Koran verse tells us that Allah cancels some of the previously revealed messages. When cancellation happens Allah brings a better revelation or a similar one.

And when we change one (sign) verse for another, and Allah knoweth best what He revealeth, they say, "Thou art only a fabricator."

The Koran, Chapter 16:104

This passage admits that the Koran has verses that have changed in message. Muhammad's critics look at the changes which are commanding opposite things and say that he is fabricating them. This is because they believe that a true word from God would not change and command opposite things. Muhammad's answer is that Allah has power over all things. In other words Allah changes his mind as he pleases.

To determine which verse is the will of Allah between two conflicting passages is a matter of figuring out which verses were given later. The later revelations by Gabriel cancel out the previous ones, and are thus, the revelations that are to be obeyed.

Verses commanding hate and violence are the winners in the cancel contest

The verses in the Koran are not in order of the time they were revealed. So the reader will find verses commanding hate and violence as well as those calling for peace mixed together throughout the book. Passages teaching peace and tolerance are believed to have come from the early days when Muhammad lived in Mecca. Verses calling for hate and violence are believed to have been revealed while Muhammad lived in Medina, which was later in his life. Therefore since the hate and violence passages came later, they cancel out the peace and tolerance verses.

One of Islam's classical reference books called *The Abrogator and the Abrogated* deals with this cancellation issue. Every chapter and verse of the Koran is examined to determine which verses have been cancelled. Out of 114 chapters in the Koran there are only 43 chapters that have not been affected by cancellation.

The issue of cancellation makes it very difficult to read the Koran and know which verses are in effect and which are not. Even among highly trained and educated Muslim scholars there is disagreement on which verses are in effect and which are cancelled. So if I am a good practicing Muslim which verses do I obey?

Do I drink wine or not? What should my attitudes and actions be towards non-Muslims? Do I hate them or love them? Do I live in tolerance and peace with my non-Muslim neighbors? Should I fight the infidels until Islam rules the world?

All of these conflicting ideas are in the Muslim Holy Writings. These ideas and commands are so opposite that they all cannot be true. One must prevail over the other. The view of many Muslim scholars is that verses commanding hate and violence are valid while those teaching tolerance and peace are canceled. The Islamic Holy Writings do contain the seeds for violence in them. It is not a matter of "misinterpreting" them. Violence is clearly commanded and taught. I will show you violence was part of how Muhammad lived.

Whatever the truth of the cancellation issue may be, there are many hate and violence commands in Muslim scriptures. A faithful follower can believe he is doing the will of Allah when he blows up your children. The mixed messages given by Muhammad are confusing and dangerous. Islam is bi-polar. Some Muslims will follow the way of peace commanded by certain verses. Others Muslims will follow the way of violence that other verses command.

There is no separation of Church and State in Islam

The teachings of the Islamic faith do not recognize a separation of Church and State. That is, Islam seeks to establish Islamic states on earth. These Islamic governments would have systems of law that conform to Muslim beliefs. This is called "Sharia Law" which is a body of Islamic religious law.

There are many countries in the world today that have Islamic states and legal systems of Sharia Law. In these countries the State and Mosque are one. If a country's population has a majority of

Muslims the chances are it will begin to move towards combining the state and the Islamic faith.

Here is an explanation, by a Muslim, of the lack of separation of church and state in Islam. These are some excerpts from an article entitled "Separation Of Church And State" written by Dr. Jaafar Sheik Idris found on www.jaafardris.com.

> *Separation of church and state is widely accepted in the West and thus has become a globally political thought.*
>
> *For these reasons, advocates of this policy of separation find that it is best if a state takes a secular approach, neither supporting nor denying any religion. It is up to the citizens to follow whatever faith and values they choose and practice what rituals they please.*
>
> *So how are Muslims to approach the modern trend of separation of religion and state in their countries? The basic belief in Islam is that the Qur'an is one hundred percent the word of God, and the Sunna was also as a result of the guidance of God to the Prophet, peace be upon him. Islam cannot be separated from the state because it guides Muslims through every detail of running the state and their lives. Muslims have no choice but to reject secularism for it excludes the laws of God.*
>
> *Secularism cannot be a solution for countries with a Muslim majority, for it requires people to replace their God-given beliefs with an entirely different set of man-made beliefs. Separation of religion and state is not an option for Muslims because is requires us to abandon God's decree for that of a man.*
>
> Dr. Jaafar Sheik Idris – www.jaafardris.com.

Sunni and Shi'a — The two main divisions of Islam

Before Muhammad died, he did not appoint a successor to his rule over the Muslims. After his death, a disagreement arose as to how a successor to the prophet should be chosen.

One group believed that Muhammad did not appoint a successor because he believed that it was best that the community of Muslims come together and choose the new ruler. This group met and selected Abu Bakr, Muhammad's trusted friend, to become the new leader. Those who agreed with this method of selecting the new leader became known as Sunni, which means "followers of the tradition of Muhammad."

The other group believed that it was Allah alone who should appoint a successor to Muhammad. Allah had appointed Muhammad to be a prophet and would likewise appoint successors to continue the Islamic rule. This group believed that Ali, Muhammad's son-in-law, was chosen by Allah to lead. This group became known as the Shi'a Muslims, which means "supporters of Ali."

These two groups, the Sunni and Shi'a, became a major division in Islam. Today, about 90 percent of Muslims are Sunni, while the remaining 10 percent are Shi'a. Over the years, these groups have fought over their differences and killed each other.

Within both the Sunni and Shi'a are moderate and extremist elements. There are Islamic terrorist groups that come from both of them.

Graduate of Islam 101

Now that you have completed this chapter you are a graduate of my Islam 101 course. I have not explained everything about Islam. They are many other books where you can get those details if you wish.

The 9/11 Verses

What I have explained is what you need to know to be able to understand the rest of this book. You now know enough of the fundamentals of Islam to be able to make sense of the quotations from the Koran and the Hadith.

In other words, you now possess the foundation you need to understand *The 9/11 Verses*.

بِسْمِ اللهِ الرَّحْمٰنِ الرَّحِيْمِ

Muslim Violence Equation

> *If you love those who love you,*
> *what reward will you get?*
> *And if you greet only your brothers*
> *what are you doing more than others?*
> **Jesus Christ**

> *O Believers! Take not infidels for friends*
> *rather than believers. Would you furnish Allah*
> *with clear right to punish you?*
> **Muhammad**

What is it about the Islamic Faith that causes thousands of acts of violence? What in the Koran and Hadith adds up to Muslims feeling justified to hurt, harm and murder people like you and me? I believe there are four main elements that when combined together result in a high level of Islamic violence. I call this the Muslim violence equation. When these four elements are combined together violence is the result.

An Attitude of hate towards non-Muslims

First there is the attitude towards non-Muslims taught by the Koran and Muhammad. Examples are given in the next chapter called "Live and Let Die." As I read the Koran, I was stunned by the anger and hate towards non-believers coming from its pages. As a child in Sunday school, I sang a song called "Jesus loves the little children." The words are at the top of the next page.

Jesus loves the little children. All the children of the world. Red and yellow, black and white. They are precious in his sight. Jesus loves the little children of the world.

This song taught in a simple way the Christian belief that God loves all mankind regardless of race or background. The life of Christ and the New Testament scriptures are filled with commands and examples to help and care for people no matter what their faith. In fact, Christians have gone all over the world giving medical care, food, housing, and clothing to people of all faiths and races. The Christian's goal is to bring non-believers to faith in Christ in part by helping and loving them.

My reading of the Koran left me with a sense that a Muslim should look at non-Muslims as worthless inferiors, to be hated and scorned. Non-believers are the enemies of Muslims. Allah does not love non-believers. When you view another human being as worthless in God's sight, then, it is a lot easier to do violent things to them.

This attitude of hate towards non-Muslims taught in the Holy Writings of Islam is the first major element in the Muslim equation for violence.

Commands to kill non-Muslims

Even more shocking are the many commands by Allah and Muhammad to kill non-believers. This is the second major element in the Muslim violence equation that leads to terrorist acts. In the chapter called "Allah Loves a Cheerful Killer," I will show you these "killing verses."

As I read these "killing passages," I reflexively compared them to the teachings of my own faith. Read the New Testament through. You will not find any hint of a command to kill non-Christians. In fact, when Peter used his sword to try and protect

Jesus, he was told to put it away. Christ told us that His kingdom is not of this world. Paul tells us that our fight is not against flesh and blood but is a spiritual fight against spiritual forces.

In the past men calling themselves Christians have certainly persecuted and killed those of other faiths. But there is absolutely no justification in the Bible or the life of Christ for doing so. As you will see there is plenty of justification for killing non-believers in the Koran and life of Muhammad.

Commands to force Islamic beliefs on non-Muslims

The third major element of my Muslim violence equation is force. The Holy Writings of Islam are filled with commands to use force against non-Muslims. Violence is threatened to get a non-believer to convert. Violence is carried out if they refuse.

The chapter "Unbelievers Turn or Burn" shows the verses that lead the Islamic faithful to force their views on non-believers. Islam claims to be superior and all mankind must live under the law of Allah. Christianity also claims to be the one true faith. But being a Christian is a voluntary choice and cannot be forced.

Once I am a Christian, I am obligated to live under the rules of my faith. I do not expect non-Christians to live by the rules of Christ. Muhammad teaches that Allah expects his followers to fight until all infidels are killed or forced to submit to Islam. The messenger of Allah also demonstrates that Islamic rules are to be followed by Muslims and non-Muslims alike.

Jesus taught that what is in your heart is what is important. Force cannot change a heart. One day, when I was a child, I got in trouble for doing something, which has been lost in the fog of 40 years of time. My mother "forced" me to sit down for a time-out punishment. In my rebellious state, I remember saying to her, "I may be sitting down, but in my heart I am still standing up."

My mother's force could not change my heart. Only my own willingness to change it could do that. True faith in God cannot come from violence and force but only from a believer's willing heart.

Promised reward of heaven for violence against non-Muslims

The last part of the Muslim equation of violence is the promise of a great reward for hurting, harming or killing non-believers. Muhammad said that the highest action you can take is to fight and kill for Allah. This guarantees the holy warrior a place in heaven. "For Me To Die Is Paradise" is the chapter that will show you the verses that teach violence for Allah brings great reward.

As I discovered these passages, I automatically compared them to my own tradition. Christianity teaches that heaven is gained by having your sins forgiven by Christ. Christ died for us so he could take our sins on himself. I cannot do anything for God to merit entrance into heaven. Islam teaches that I can do something for Allah to merit entrance into paradise. I can understand why so many followers answer the call to violence when the reward is so great.

Four major elements of Islam cause violence

I believe these four elements of Islam directly explain the 11,098 acts of religious inspired violence committed by Muslims since 9/11. Recently, a non-Muslim teacher from England working in the Sudan was convicted of "insulting the prophet" because she allowed her students to name a teddy bear Muhammad. Muslim protesters in the street demanded that she be killed for her "crime."

These Muslims believe they have the right to force their religious views on non-Muslims even to the point of death. But how can they be blamed? They are just following the words and life of the prophet Muhammad. The prophet had many people killed for "insulting him." Muhammad forced his views on others and so they did as they saw their prophet do.

The messenger of Allah demanded the death penalty for many "crimes" including: drinking alcohol, homosexuality, adultery and insulting Allah. I guess Muhammad would have had Jesus killed or punished for performing his first miracle. Changing water into wine at a wedding is just not Allah's will.

Amber Pawlik wrote an interesting piece called *Islam on Trial: The Prosecution's Case against Islam*. At www.amberpawlik.com you can read it for yourself. Amber wanted to determine a percentage estimate of how much of the Koran's subject matter was about non-Muslims. She also wanted to determine statistically what the Koran's tone was towards non-believers. So Amber performed a scientific statistical study of the verses in the Koran.

Her conclusion was that 52.7 percent of the verses in the Koran are hatred aimed at infidels. I am not surprised by her findings. I got the same impression after reading the Koran even without examining the verses statistically. Our Muslim violence equation says there is a strong negative push in Islam against non-Muslims. Amber's research confirms this statistically.

Muslim violence equation proven true

There are two types of moderate Muslims, those who ignore parts of Islam and those who want to reform parts of it. In the last chapter you will be able to learn more about moderate Muslims. Both types of moderate Muslims prove the truth of our Muslim violence equation. Those Muslims who ignore the violent *9/11 Verses* are acknowledging that Islam can only be a "religion of peace" without these verses.

In the same way, the reformists are conceding that Islam can only be a "religion of peace" without the violent passages that they want to eliminate. In either case the Muslim violence equation is proven true. The next four chapters will examine each of the four major elements in Islam that lead to violence. Read the verses, the sayings and doings of Muhammad, and see if you agree that they are *The 9/11 Verses*.

The Muslim violence equation – The four major elements of Islam that create violence

Islamic Violence is caused by:

- An Attitude of hate towards non-Muslims

- Commands to kill non-Muslims

- Commands to force Islamic beliefs on non-Muslims

- Promised Reward of Heaven for violence against non-Muslims

بِسْمِ اللهِ الرَّحْمٰنِ الرَّحِيمِ
Live and Let Die

> The Lord is not slow in keeping his promise, as some understand slowness. He is patient with you, not wanting anyone to perish, but everyone to come to repentance.
>
> **The Apostle Peter**

> Let not the infidels deem that the length of days we give them is good for them! We only give them length of days that they may increase their sins! And a shameful chastisement shall be their lot.
>
> **Allah**

> You see, at just the right time, when we were still powerless, Christ died for the ungodly. Very rarely will anyone die for a righteous man, though for a good man someone might possibly dare to die. But God demonstrates his own love for us in this: While we were yet sinners, Christ died for us.
>
> **The Apostle Paul**

> Obey Allah and the Apostle; but if ye turn away, then verily, Allah loveth not the unbelievers.
>
> **Muhammad**

Attitude matters

The attitude a faith has towards those who are outside it matters. An attitude of hate towards non-Muslims is the first of the four main elements of Islam that lead to acts like 9/11. The quote at the beginning of this chapter shows the attitude that the God of the Bible has towards unbelievers. He is patient with those who do evil and does not want anyone to perish. Instead God wants those who do evil to turn around their lives (repent) and do good. God gives people time so that they have the opportunity to come to repentance and live rightly. God loves unbelievers.

The next quote shows the attitude of Allah in the Koran. He gives unbelievers time so they have an opportunity to sin more. Allah does this not for their good, but so they can pile up more sins for a future greater punishment. Allah loveth not the unbelievers.

The amount of hate and contempt that the Islamic Holy Writings show towards unbelievers is shocking. A faith can believe it is true and still show caring and concern for those outside it. Through *The 9/11 Verses*, Islam shows no love for outsiders.

Christianity views those outside the faith are as "lost" and in "darkness." They are considered by Christian believers with sympathy. Unbelievers are in need of the light and love of God. The Bible says "there will be more rejoicing in heaven over one sinner that repents than over ninety-nine righteous persons who do not need to repent." This shows that God cares about the unbeliever. The Christian is to be a helpful guide to the unbeliever.

Islam puts up a solid wall of negative attitude between Muslims and non-Muslims. Islamic writings have an attitude of hate and contempt towards non-believers. This attitude is reflected in the actions of modern followers of Allah. Since "Allah loveth not the unbelievers" then those who worship Allah should likewise hate the infidel. The Muslim who saws off the head of an "infidel" is just hating unbelievers as Allah does.

It is easy to hate those who are not like you. For thousands of years of human history, mankind has loved their own "tribe" and hated and fought those from other tribes. Human beings have many differences. Race, geography, language, culture and religion are some of the main ones. It would seem our differences make it easy to think of others as less human than we are.

Live and let die

The United States was founded on the concept of live and let live. In matters of faith this means that we leave each other alone. People have the freedom to practice faith as they believe they should. Instead of live and let live, Muhammad's teaching is more like live and let die. Look at this quote from the Koran.

Believers! wage war against such of the infidels as are your neighbors, and let them find you rigorous: and know that Allah is with those who fear him.
The Koran, Chapter 9:123

Can you see from this passage how a Muslim terrorist can feel justified in taking action against infidels? Allah's attitude is not to save the unbeliever but to destroy him. Look at the attitude displayed by Muhammad in this description of his actions as he killed for Allah.

☪

Muslim Hadith Book 19, number 4457

The Messenger of Allah (may peace be upon him) used not to kill the children, so thou shouldst not kill them unless... you could distinguish between a child who would grow up to be a

*believer (and a child who would grow up to be a non-believer),
so that you killed the (prospective) non-believer and left the
(prospective) believer aside.*

Stop and think about this for a minute. Muhammad is
teaching that if it were possible to know which children are going
to grow up and not be Muslim then it would be okay to kill them.
What does this say about the value and worth of non-Muslims?
What attitude does this teaching instill into Muslims young and
old?

Muhammad killed the men who were not Muslim. What kind
of message does this send about Allah's attitude towards
unbelievers? The surviving children and wives were considered
property to be distributed to the Muslim fighters. These wives and
children then became slaves of the Muslims.

The only good friend is a Muslim friend

*O believers! Take not infidels for friends rather than believers.
Would you furnish Allah with clear right to punish you?*
The Koran, Chapter 4:143

*They desire that ye should be infidels that ye should be alike.
Take therefore none of them for friends, till they have fled
their homes for the cause of Allah. If they turn back, then seize
them, and slay them wherever ye find them...*
The Koran, Chapter 4:91

*O believers! take not the Jews or Christians as friends. They are
but one another's friends. If any one taketh them for his*

friends, he surely is one of them! Allah will not guide the evil doers. **The Koran, Chapter 5:56**

The Koran teaches that Allah will punish you if you take Jews or Christians as friends. If you have a Jewish or Christian friend then you are one of them. Again, the message instilled in Allah's followers is an attitude of contempt for all non-Muslims who are classified as "evil doers." A good Muslim is to stay away from these infidels.

The founder of my faith was criticized for associating with "evil doers." The Jewish religious leaders called Jesus a "friend of sinners." His response to them was "it is not those who are well that need a doctor, but those who are sick." The attitude of Christ was to offer his love and forgiveness to "evil doers" who desperately needed it. This shows that God cares for those who are living lives far away from him. Allah and his followers are no "friend of sinners."

The Koran, Chapter 4:91, describes the Islamic practice of driving non-Muslims out of their homes to insure that the only religion being practiced is Islam. These verses are not just an out-of-date command from hundreds of years ago. Modern Muslims still act on attitudes drawn from the Holy Writings of Islam. Here are some excerpts from a February 01, 2006 report from Iraq entitled, "Bombs, But Also Hidden Persecution to Drive Christians Out of Iraq" found at www.asianews.it.

Mosul (AsiaNews) – There is a "hidden reality of persecution" against Iraq's Christians, including daily threats, kidnappings, discrimination and at its worst bomb attacks, such as ... a series of car bombings against Christian places of worship in Kirkuk and Baghdad. The aim: to feed internal divisions and the ongoing political instability, but also to "drive the Christian community out of Iraq."

39

The 9/11 Verses

The article goes on to explain that in 2004 Muslims attacked four churches in Baghdad and three churches in Mosul. These terrorist acts caused the death of 12 people while dozens were left injured. The attacks were well planned and the weapons used were car bombs. The bishop over the Chaldean church sees these attacks as part of an ongoing effort by Muslims to force Christians to leave Iraq.

In Mosul, Christians are kidnapped and held for ransom. Many in the Christian community are choosing to leave rather than expose their families to the danger. Towards the end of the article the following observation is made. I believe this gives an informative insight into the attitude that Muslims have towards non-Muslims.

> *Categorically leaving aside the possibility that a future Iraqi government could drift towards fundamentalism, some local seminarians tell us that Christians are "more or less used to being discriminated against. On the streets, in the city, they always throw the same accusations at us: 'infidels of the cross'. Even with Muslims with whom we are on good terms we always feel the weight of this condemnation."*
> **www.asianews.it**— 02/01/06

Many Muslims in Iraq including the top spiritual leader have condemned these attacks on Christians. Average Muslims have shown caring and concern for Christians who are being hurt. However, what can a Muslim say to those who read these verses and are taking them seriously and following them? How can they deny that Muhammad did drive Christians and Jews out of "Muslim lands." The so-called "radical Islamists" are just following what the Holy Writings of Islam teach.

Show no kindness to infidels (non-Muslims)

O ye who believe! Take not My foe and your foe for friends, shewing them kindness, although they believe not the truth which hath come to you: they drive forth the apostles and yourselves because ye believe in Allah your Lord! If you go forth to fight on My way, and from a desire to please Me, and shew them kindness in private, I well know what you conceal, and what ye discover! Whoso doth this hath already gone astray from even the way.   The Koran, Chapter 60:1

Muhammad is the Apostle of Allah; and his comrades are vehement against the infidels, but full of tenderness among themselves.   The Koran, Chapter 48:8

…Verily, the infidels are your undoubted enemies!
The Koran, Chapter 4:102

As I read these verses, I recalled the teaching of the Apostle Paul. Paul says God shows his kindness to all people (both the good and evil) by giving them food, drink and all the many joys of life. In the book of Romans, the Apostle Paul says that God is kind to non-believers, hoping that those who are living their lives in sin will change and live for God.

Allah has a much different attitude. These verses clearly show He does not want kindness to be shown outside his own "tribe" of Muslims.

Most people I know instinctively would show kindness to someone in need regardless of the person's faith. Our family, through World Vision, a Christian aid organization, has supported several poor children around the World for many years. In 1993,

41

we started supporting a three-year-old girl in the Philippines. Her family was very poor and her mother extremely ill.

The first picture we received of her shows a thin girl who looks unhappy and malnourished. Each year, World Vision sends a new picture and a progress report. It was amazing to see the transformation of this girl into a smiling, healthy young lady. She has done well in school and is getting ready to go to college soon. World Vision encourages correspondence between sponsor and child. In one of her letters to us she wrote, "without your help I cannot achieve my dreams."

All people around the world have dreams. Because we are all created in the image of God we have worth. Everyone should have the opportunity to have dreams and go after them.

I work very hard to support my family. What would motivate and inspire my wife and I to part with money that is ours to show kindness to a girl halfway around the world who we do not even know? The answer is love. This love was taught and lived by the founder of our faith. I want to have the same attitude of kindness and love that Christ had.

Have we ever asked what faith the children we help are? No. Does World Vision only help Christians? No. In fact for several years we supported a girl who lives in Gaza. She attends the local Mosque. The pictures World Vision sent show her wearing traditional Islamic clothing. What faith do you think she is?

All homosexuals are to be killed

This next verse is short and to the point. Muhammad, should we live and let live with homosexuals?

Muslim Hadith Book 38, Number 4447
Narrated by Abdullah ibn Abbas

The Prophet (peace be upon him) said: If you find anyone doing as Lot's people did, kill the one who does it, and the one to whom it is done.

Lot's story is told in the book of Genesis in the Bible. He was the nephew of Abraham. Lot and his family lived in a town called Sodom. The people of Sodom were known for their homosexuality. This is where we get the word "sodomy" to describe a certain sexual act. This quote from Muhammad institutes the death penalty for those caught in homosexual acts.

Modern Muslim countries such as Iran and Saudi Arabia punish and execute homosexuals just as Muhammad commanded. According to a United Nations report, thousands of homosexuals have been executed in Saudi Arabia. Saudi Arabia lives under Islamic law. Clearly Islamic law according to Muhammad calls for all homosexuals to be killed.

According to Iran's top religious leader, the Grand Ayatollah Al-Sistani, homosexuals should be killed "in the worst possible manner." Other Muslim religious leaders and jurists have executed homosexuals by beheading them, throwing them off the tallest building in the city or placing them in a pit next to a wall and toppling the wall on them to bury them alive. Taliban leader, Mullah Mohammad Omar, was present at the execution of three homosexual men who were buried alive by toppled walls.

Christianity condemns homosexual acts but does not prescribe in its Holy Writings any earthly penalty for the state to enact against homosexuals. Governments in primarily Christian nations have created laws against homosexuals, but these came from other considerations. There are no specific New Testament Biblical commands to outlaw the practice. Laws against homosexual acts pre-date Christianity by at least 1000 years. The Middle Assyrian Law codes (1075 BC) state: "If a man have intercourse with his brother-in-arms, they shall turn him into a eunuch" (castrate him).

The attitude of Islam towards homosexuals is another example of the faiths inability to live and let live.

The Islamic 4-step program

I enjoy a good drink. Some people I know drink adult beverages while others do not. People enjoy or abstain from alcohol for a variety of reasons including religious beliefs. Everyone I know has an attitude of live and let live when it comes to drinking. Islam is totally intolerant of alcoholic beverages.

You might say that Muhammad had a four-step program to cure the alcoholic. Step one beat the daylights out of the drinker. If he drinks again, follow step two, which is to beat the holy daylights out of him. For a third time offense of drinking, use step three, which is beating the living daylights out of him. Step four cures the drinker once and for all. Kill him. I am not making this stuff up. Here is the quote from the Hadith.

Muslim Hadith Book 38, Number 4469
Narrated by AbuHurayrah

The Prophet (peace be upon him) said: If he is intoxicated, flog him; again if he is intoxicated, flog him; again if he is intoxicated, flog him, if he does it again a fourth time, kill him.

Muhammad lays down a strict law prohibiting Alcohol. This law applies to everyone even those who are not Muslim. There is no live and let live with this issue.

Saudi Arabia has made Islam the law of the land. On February 5, 2007 www.foxnews.com carried an associated press report entitled "Saudi Court Orders Lashing, Jail for 20 Foreigners for Drinking, Dancing at Mixed Party." The article, out of Riyadh Saudi Arabia, discusses a recent court case. The Saudi religious police had arrested foreigners for drinking alcohol and mixed gender dancing at a party.

In Saudi Arabia the religious police patrol public places in the country looking for violations of Islamic law. Even law that is based only on religious considerations must be followed by non-Muslim foreigners. Men and women speaking to each other at a party is a violation of the law. Drinking alcohol, as we have already read in the Koran, is against Islamic Law as well.

The arrested foreigners were tried and convicted. The judge sentenced them to prison terms ranging from three to four months. They also were given lashes as required by the Koran.

These 20 convictions are just the start since 433 people in total were arrested. The others were awaiting trial at the time of the conviction of the first 20. By way of explanation the article reports that Saudi Arabia follows a "strict interpretation" of Islam which "bans alcohol and meetings between unrelated men and women."

I disagree with the article's explanation that Saudi Arabia follows a "strict interpretation" of Islam. You do not need a "strict interpretation" of Islam to ban alcohol and meetings between unrelated men and women. The Prophet Muhammad clearly established these laws. Muslims who do not follow them are ignoring the prophet. Saudi Arabia is just following the Islamic law that Muhammad taught. In Iraq, Saddam's government used to grant permits to sell alcohol to non-Muslims. But Muhammad would not have agreed with this.

Let all the land be Muslim

Muslim Hadith Book 019, Number 4366

It has been narrated by 'Umar b. al-Khattib that he heard the Messenger of Allah (may peace be upon him) say: I will expel the Jews and Christians from the Arabian Peninsula and will not leave any but Muslim.

Here is another example of the prophet's unwillingness to live and let live. Muhammad first preaches his message to the Jews and Christians. When they rejected his call to convert, he expelled or killed them. Mitchel Bard in a piece entitled "The Treatment of Jews in Arab/Islamic Countries," found at www.jewishvirtual library.org, describes some of the history about the expelling of the Jews.

Muhammad, the founder of Islam, traveled to Medina in 622 A.D. to attract followers to his new faith. When the Jews of Medina refused to convert and rejected Muhammad, two of the major Jewish tribes were expelled; in 627, Muhammad's followers killed between 600 and 900 of the men, and divided the surviving Jewish women and children amongst themselves.

The Muslim attitude toward Jews is reflected in various verses throughout the Koran, the holy book of the Islamic faith. "They [the Children of Israel] were consigned to humiliation and wretchedness. They brought the wrath of God upon themselves, and this because they used to deny God's signs and kill His Prophets unjustly and because they disobeyed and were transgressors" (Sura 2:61).

According to the Koran, the Jews try to introduce corruption (5:64), have always been disobedient (5:78), and are enemies of Allah, the Prophet and the angels (2:97 98).

Mitchell Bard
www.jewishvirtuallibrary.org

Those defending Islam say that Jews and Christians were allowed to "live in peace" in Islamic lands. Bard in his piece discusses this.

Still, as "People of the Book," Jews (and Christians) are protected under Islamic law. The traditional concept of the "dhimma" ("writ of protection") was extended by Muslim conquerors to Christians and Jews in exchange for their subordination to the Muslims. Peoples subjected to Muslim rule usually had a choice between death and conversion, but Jews and Christians, who adhered to the Scriptures, were allowed as dhimmis (protected persons) to practice their faith.

This "protection" did little, however, to insure that Jews and Christians were treated well by the Muslims. On the contrary, an integral aspect of the dhimma was that, being an infidel, he had to openly acknowledge the superiority of the true believer—the Muslim.

In the early years of the Islamic conquest, the "tribute" (or jizya), paid as a yearly poll tax, symbolized the subordination of the dhimmi. Later, the inferior status of Jews and Christians was reinforced through a series of regulations that governed the behavior of the dhimmi. Dhimmis, on pain of death, were forbidden to mock or criticize the Koran, Islam or Muhammad, to proselytize among Muslims or to touch a Muslim woman (though a Muslim man could take a non Muslim as a wife).

Dhimmis were excluded from public office and armed service, and were forbidden to bear arms. They were not allowed to ride horses or camels, to build synagogues or churches taller than mosques, to construct houses higher than those of Muslims or to drink wine in public. They were not allowed to pray or mourn in loud voices—as that might offend the Muslims. The dhimmi had to show public deference toward Muslims—always yielding them the center of the road. The dhimmi was not allowed to give evidence in court against a Muslim, and his oath was unacceptable in an Islamic court. To defend himself, the dhimmi would have to purchase Muslim witnesses at great expense. This left the dhimmi with little legal recourse when harmed by a Muslim.

Dhimmis were also forced to wear distinctive clothing. In the ninth century, for example, Baghdad's Caliph al-Mutawakkil designated a yellow badge for Jews, setting a precedent that would be followed centuries later in Nazi Germany.

Mitchell Bard
www.jewishvirtuallibrary.org

Before I examined the Holy Writings of Islam, I would read statements from Muslims saying that Islam lived at peace with other faiths. Perhaps you have read these statements in your local newspaper or have heard them on your television or radio. Peaceful living with other faiths can take different forms. True peace happens when different faiths can live side by side without one faith forcing others to act according to their views. This is a peace built on the concept of live and let live.

Muslim countries today still enact laws that show an attitude of contempt for those of other faiths. In these countries criticizing Islam or making fun of some aspect of the faith can earn you a death sentence. In the land of Islam your income and social status will probably be severely reduced if you are not Muslim.

Majorities tend to oppress minorities. This seems to be built into our human nature. Young children exhibit this behavior. They pick on and tease other children who act and look different.

By making acts of oppression a command of Allah, Islam lends credibility to the majorities persecution of unbelievers.

There is no such thing as "innocent" non-Muslim women and children

Bukhari Hadith Volume 4, Book 52, Number 256
Narrated by As-Sab bin Jaththama

The Prophet passed by me at a place called Al-Abwa or Waddan, and was asked whether it was permissible to attack the pagan warriors at night with the probability of exposing their women and children to danger. The Prophet replied, "They (i.e. women and children) are from them (i.e. pagans)."

Here, Muhammad's Jihad warriors ask a compassionate question about exposing non-combatants to being hurt or killed in the fighting. The messenger of Allah answers that the exposure of women and children to danger in the attack is permissible since "they are from the pagans. " Can you see how this attitude can cause a follower of Muhammad to blow up civilians?

When you hear Muslims saying that Islam forbids the killing of "innocents" remember that it all depends on what the meaning of the word "innocent" is.

Muhammad's true attitude towards Jews and Christians

When I read these next three Hadith passages, I was amazed. Muhammad is speaking about the Day of Resurrection when all people will be judged by Allah to determine whether they will spend eternity in heaven or hell. In order to admit Muslims to heaven, Allah takes Jews and Christians and throws them into hell. Jews and Christians are sacrificed for Muslims. The prophets true regard and attitude towards Jews and Christians comes through loud and clear.

Muslim Hadith Book 037, Number 6665

Abu Musa' reported that Allah's Messenger (may peace be upon him) said: When it will be the Day of Resurrection Allah would deliver to every Muslim a Jew or a Christian and say: That is your rescue from Hell-Fire.

Muslim Hadith Book 037, Number 6666

Abu Burda reported on the authority of his father that Allah's Apostle (may peace be upon him) said: No Muslim would die, but Allah would admit in his stead a Jew or a Christian in Hell-Fire.

Muslim Hadith Book 037, Number 6668

Abu Burda reported Allah's Messenger (may peace be upon him) as saying: There would come people amongst the Muslims on the Day of Resurrection with as heavy sins as a mountain, and Allah would forgive them and He would place in their stead the Jews and the Christians.

Religious pride does not please God

Christian scriptures caution the believer not to think of themselves as superior to others. In the story of the Pharisee and the tax collector Jesus makes this point.

✝

To some who were confident of their own righteousness and looked down on everybody else, Jesus told this parable: "Two men went up to the temple to pray, one a Pharisee and the other a tax collector. The Pharisee stood up and prayed about himself: 'God, I thank you that I am not like other men—robbers, evildoers, adulterers—or even like this tax collector. I fast twice a week and give a tenth of all I get.' But the tax collector stood at a distance. He would not even look up to Heaven, but beat his breast and said, 'God, have mercy on me a sinner.' I tell you this man, rather than the other, went home justified before God. For everyone who exalts himself will be humbled, and he who humbles himself will be exalted."   John 18:9-14

The Pharisees were the most religious Jews of their time. Tax collectors were considered to be very evil sinners by Jewish society. Yet the Pharisee in his prayer just went on and on to God about how good and superior he was to others. The "evil doer" tax collector asked for God's mercy admitting he was a sinner. The tax collector was given mercy and forgiveness from God because he humbled himself and admitted that he was a sinner in great need of God's mercy. The Pharisee who bragged about himself did not get forgiveness and mercy. He did not think he needed it. He believed he was superior.

The pride of Islam

The Islamic attitude that we have studied in this chapter is not unlike that of the Pharisee. There seems to be a sense of superiority in Muhammad and his followers.

In July 2007, Hassan Butt, a former Islamic Jihadist, posted an article at www.dailymail.co.uk entitled "I was a fanatic...I know their thinking, says former radical Islamist." Mr. Butt shows very well the attitude of superiority that Islamic terrorists have toward the non-Muslim world. The real cause of the Jihadist's attitude is Islamic theology, which comes out of the Koran and Hadith passages I have shown you.

The 9/11 Verses

Mr. Butt was a member of a network of Jihadists operating out of the United Kingdom. He and his fellow Jihadists would laugh when the British media would declare that the causes for 9/11 and other terrorist attacks were the policies of the Western governments. Hassan knew that the real cause of the terrorist violence he was engaging in was Islamic theology.

Mr. Butt disagrees completely with those in the United Kingdom, such as the mayor of London, who stated that the London subway bombings happened because young Muslims were disaffected by the war in Iraq.

Hassan quit the terror network in February 2006 because he believed that his associates had become "mindless killers." Here are some excerpts from the article that give a window into the thoughts of these terrorists.

> *If we were interested in justice, you may ask, how did this continuing violence come to be the means of promoting such a (flawed) Utopian goal? How do Islamic radicals justify such terror in the name of their religion? There isn't enough room to outline everything here, but the foundation of extremist reasoning rests upon a model of the world in which you are either a believer or an infidel.*
>
> *Formal Islamic theology, unlike Christian theology, does not allow for the separation of state and religion: they are considered to be one and the same. For centuries, the reasoning of Islamic jurists has set down rules of interaction between Dar ul-Islam (the Land of Islam) and Dar ul-Kufr (the Land of Unbelief) to cover almost every matter of trade, peace and war. But what radicals and extremists do is to take this two steps further.*
>
> *Their first step has been to argue that, since there is no pure Islamic state, the whole world must be Dar ul-Kufr (The Land of Unbelief). Step two: since Islam must declare war on*

unbelief, they have declared war upon the whole world. Along with many of my former peers, I was taught by Pakistani and British radical preachers that this reclassification of the globe as a Land of War (Dar ul-Harb) allows any Muslim to destroy the sanctity of the five rights that every human is granted under Islam: life, wealth, land, mind and belief. In Dar ul-Harb, anything goes, including the treachery and cowardice of attacking civilians.

In this theology, the non-Muslim world is viewed as a place where anything goes. Unbelievers are not given the rights to life, wealth, land, mind and belief that are given to believers. The land of Islam is superior to the land of unbelief. This allows the terrorist to hurt the innocent since they are just worthless unbelievers who are outside the superiority of Islam. The Muslim terrorist can commit horrible acts and still sleep well at night.

This theology would not be possible without verses in the Koran and the life of Muhammad to support it. The Muslim creators of this theology do not need to take the verses out of context. They do not need to twist and turn them to make them say what they want.

Could this theology of hate towards non-Muslims be created if Muhammad had the following attitude and lived his life by it?

✝

You have heard that it was said, 'Love your neighbor and hate your enemy.' But I tell you: Love your enemies and pray for those who persecute you, that you may be sons of your Father in heaven. He causes his sun to rise on the evil and the good, and sends rain on the righteous and the unrighteous. If you love those who love you, what reward will you get? Are not even the tax collectors doing that? And if you greet only your brothers, what are you doing more than others? Do not even

*pagans do that? Be perfect, therefore, as your heavenly Father
is perfect.*   **Matthew 5:43-48**

This teaching by Jesus is a direct reflection of God's attitude towards those who are outside the faith. The purpose of loving your enemy is to one day be able to call them your friend. God's example is that he loved us and Christ died for mankind while we were still his enemies. Now God is able to call those who love him his friends. This is our example to live by with our own enemies.

Live and let live is not the attitude of the Holy Writings of Islam. Live and let die is. This dying can be in the form of physical death or the daily death of living under the rule of a faith that views you as inferior. There is in all of us the capacity to think that we are superior to others who are different. Human history both ancient and modern is full of examples of this part of Human nature. The way blacks in the United States were treated when slavery was legal and even after the civil war is similar to treatment of non-Muslims under Islam.

Many times people claim to represent a faith but do not practice it correctly. Unfortunately, this attitude of superiority and the willingness to do violence to others is a clear part of the Holy Writings of Islam. The attitude that a faith has towards those outside it really does matter.

Life in the land of the "religion of peace"

I want to close this chapter with some modern stories of what it is like to live in places where Islam is taken seriously. This is what happens to non-Muslims when Allah's faithful believe and live by the attitude towards non-believers that Islam teaches.

The following quote is from an excerpt of an Interview entitled "Symposium: The Muslim Persecution of Christians" by Jamie Glazov appearing in www.frontpagemagazine.com on 10/10/2003.

Live and Let Die

Paul Marshall, a Senior Fellow at Freedom House's Center For Religious Freedom, answers the question by the moderator.

Question: *Welcome to Frontpage Symposium ladies and gentlemen. Let's begin with the question that will build a foundation to this discussion: how widespread is the persecution of Christians in the Islamic world?*

Answer: *Very widespread, there are few Muslim countries where it does not occur. It takes four forms. First. there are direct, violent attacks by extremists on Christian communities. These occur in Egypt, Algeria, Iran, Yemen, Pakistan, Bangladesh, the Philippines, Nigeria, Indonesia (the list is not exhaustive). In most of these cases the Government is either unable or unwilling to stop the attacks.*

Second, there is civil war and communal violence where the Christian community has resisted the spread of radical varieties of Islam. Since the National Islamic Front (formerly the Muslim Brotherhood) took power in Sudan in the late 1980s two million people have been killed, mostly Christians and animists. In Nigeria some 11,000 people have been killed in the last three years over the introduction of Islamic sharia law. There is a similar death toll in eastern Indonesia, where paramilitary militant organizations such as Laskar Jihad, allied to international terrorists, have slaughtered local populations.

Third, there is widespread discrimination against Christians in Muslim countries. They are frequently at a disadvantage in marriage, custody and inheritance cases, are forced to subsidize Islam through taxes, are severely restricted in building and repairing churches, and are often excluded from government positions. This happens in most Muslim countries. In some cases, as in Pakistan or Iran or Nigeria, the testimony of a Christian counts less in a court case.

Fourthly, blasphemy and apostasy laws disproportionately target minorities. In Saudi Arabia, Christianity is entirely forbidden.

These next four stories found at www.bible.ca, are all from a report called "The Unveiling Of Pakistan," dated January 2000. The author is unknown. This is what can happen to non-Muslims when they are ruled over by people who have an attitude of superiority.

Do not speak against the superior faith

On 6 January 1992, Niamat Ahmar, a Christian Punjabi teacher and poet, was stabbed in the stomach and murdered by a Muslim fanatic right on the grounds of the District Education Office in Faisalabad. The reason: he was accused by another teacher with whom he had quarreled of blaspheming Muhammad, the prophet of Islam.

This accusation, though false, spread throughout the area; and the man who killed Ahmar proudly confessed to it. It was reported that when the police came, they congratulated the killer, saying that he would be in paradise for this act.

Ahmar left behind his widow, five children, his aging parents, and a young brother, all of whom were dependent upon him. Now his brother is trying to support them all; the children have been forced to stop their studies and find some sort of employment.

"The Unveiling Of Pakistan" www.bible.ca

This is what it is like to be a Christian in Pakistan—with the threat of a blasphemy allegation always hanging over one's head. The penalty is death, whether sentenced by a court or not.

Blasphemy laws used to imprison Christians

On 4 December 1999, these two brothers appeared in Court in Gujranwala, an area in the Punjab province known for its fanaticism. Both stand charged with blasphemy under Article 295C, charges that arose from a dispute involving just Saleem.

Saleem went to buy ice cream from a vendor who was a Muslim. The vendor told Saleem that he would not give him any utensils with which to eat the ice cream because Saleem was a Christian and thus was not going to use a Muslim's utensils. Eventually a scuffle occurred, and out of that day came a charge of blasphemy against both brothers, although Rasheed never was present. Actually prior to that day, there had been a land dispute involving some of the Muslim villagers and the brothers; but that had been over months earlier.

Saleem Masih is 35 years old, is married and has five children. Rasheed Masih is 45 years old, is married and has eight children. Both have been in jail, awaiting trial, since 3 June 1999. Neither can get bail. Because these are blasphemy cases, the judge refuses to release the brothers. Neither has seen his family since his arrest because the family members are too afraid of the Muslim fanatics to come to the jail to visit. The families are without any support, save for one other brother who is trying to provide for all of them.

"The Unveiling Of Pakistan" www.bible.ca

Young Christian girl treated as a slave

Nazia is a young girl from a very poor family, so poor that the children were unable to attend school. So Nazia took a job in a factory, a place from which her Muslim foreman abducted her.

For some six months she was forced to live in his house with his family, often being locked up inside the house. He took her to a mosque and threatened to kill her and all her family if she did not convert to Islam. Because she was afraid for her family, she did repeat the Islamic creed, which is all that is needed to be called a Muslim.

She also signed a document, presumably a marriage contract, for after this, it was determined that she was married to this foreman. With this, she allegedly converted to Islam and she was married to the foreman, all against her will.

By building up trust with one of his brothers, Nazia finally was able to get away. Having very carefully saved one rupee at a time, she was able to save 50 rupees (approximately $1.00 USD), enough for a "taxi" (like a rickshaw), and in November 1999, she got back to her parents. The foreman's brothers began threatening her, and she became quite frightened. A village elder helped her find legal help.

At a court hearing on 30 November 1999, with a mere wave of his hand indicating she was to leave the courtroom, the judge determined that Nazia was not forced to go with the man—that she had gone with consent—and so she had to be returned to him since he has petitioned for restoration of his conjugal rights. No evidence was presented at the hearing, save for the facts stated in her petition for divorce. Thus, she remains in hiding. All she wants is to be a Christian and live a normal life, the latter of which appears most unlikely.

"The Unveiling Of Pakistan" www.bible.ca

You have no right to your children if you are an infidel

A particularly egregious case of forced conversion concerns the three young daughters of Khushi and Seema Masih: Nadia,

Naima and Nabila. Claiming that the three girls had "embraced Islam," and thus no longer could live with Christian parents, policemen came to the Masih home and took away the daughters. This was 25 January 1998.

The Masih family rented a portion of a house from a Muslim named Liaqat Butt. There were eleven children in the family; six were married, but five were still at home. None attended school. Khushi worked as a bus driver. Seema was employed as a domestic servant, and the three girls often went with her to help. The girls were befriended by the landlord's wife, and the three began to insist that they stay at home rather than go with Seema.

It was three months later when the policemen, a social worker, the landlady and several others showed up at the door and took away Khushi and Seema's three daughters.

Khushi Masih went directly to the police station, demanding the daughters be handed over to him. He was denied custody, however; in fact the officer in charge at the station filed an application with the Assistant Commissioner stating that the three girls had "embraced Islam" and should be given over to the custody of Muslims who wanted to adopt them. The girls were sent to a group home, pending the outcome of the application.

The parents tried to see them there but were denied. However, the imam of the local mosque, the Muslim landlady and other Muslims from a religious political party were allowed to meet with the girls. When they finally were brought before a magistrate, he ordered them to stay in the group home, stating, "The girls are under pressure, and they cannot be given into the custody of their parents."
"The Unveiling Of Pakistan" www.bible.ca

The 9/11 Verses

بِسْمِ اللهِ الرَّحْمٰنِ الرَّحِيْمِ

Allah Loves a Cheerful Killer

> *My kingdom is not of this world. If it were,*
> *my servants would fight to prevent my arrest.*
> **Jesus Christ**

> *I am commanded to fight with men till they testify*
> *that there is no god but Allah, and that Muhammad is*
> *His servant and His Apostle, face our qiblah (direction*
> *of prayer), eat what we slaughter, and pray like us.*
> *When they do that, their life and property are unlawful*
> *for us except what is due to them. They will have the*
> *same rights as the Muslims have, and have the same*
> *responsibilities as the Muslims have.*
> **Muhammad**

Commands that direct the followers of Islam to kill is the second major element of the faith that cause acts like 9/11. Decrees for killing and violence leap from the pages of the Holy Writings of Islam. Within the Koran and in the actions and words of Muhammad is a fiery intense thirst for blood. You do not have to stretch or twist Islamic passages to make them command killing. They are clear and understandable.

For a terrorist, there are more than enough instructions to kill in order to feel comfortable with what he is doing. I have already discussed in the chapter "Islam 101" the bi-polar nature of Islam.

61

There are passages that call for peace and tolerance and others that command killing. Scholars can argue over which passages Muslims should believe in and practice. Just the fact that there are any passages at all that call for violence for Allah, give the killer the justification he needs.

This next story from the Hadith is a bit long, but it shows what Muhammad would do if you "insult" Allah or him. This story is a true account and really gives an insight into the minds of Muhammad and his followers.

Kill those who insult Muhammad or Allah

Muslim Hadith Book 019, Number 4436

It has been narrated on the authority of Jabir that the Messenger of Allah (may peace be upon him) said: Who will kill Ka'b b. Ashraf? He has maligned Allah, the Exalted, and His Messenger. Muhammad b. Maslama said: Messenger of Allah, do you wish that I should kill him? He said: Yes. He said: Permit me to talk (to him in the way I deem fit). He said: Talk (as you like).

So, Muhammad b. Maslama came to Ka'b and talked to him, referred to the old friendship between them and said: This man (i.e. the Holy Prophet) has made up his mind to collect charity (from us) and this has put us to a great hardship. When he heard this, Ka'b said: By God, you will be put to more trouble by him. Muhammad b. Maslama said: No doubt, now we have become his followers and we do not like to forsake him until we see what turn his affairs will take. I want that you should give me a loan.

He said: What will you mortgage? He said: What do you want? He said: Pledge me your women. He said: You are the most handsome of the Arabs; should we pledge our women to you? He said: Pledge me your children. He said: The son of one of us may abuse us saying that he was pledged for two wasqs (300lbs) of dates, but we can pledge you (cur) weapons. He said: All right.

Then Muhammad b. Maslama promised that he would come to him with Harith, Abu 'Abs b. Jabr and Abbad b. Bishr. So they came and called upon him at night. He came down to them. Sufyan says that all the narrators except 'Amr have stated that his wife said: I hear a voice which sounds like the voice of murder. He said: It is only Muhammad b. Maslama and his foster-brother, Abu Na'ila. When a gentleman is called at night even if to be pierced with a spear, he should respond to the call.

Muhammad said to his companions: As he comes down, I will extend my hands towards his head and when I hold him fast, you should do your job. So when he came down and he was holding his cloak under his arm, they said to him: We sense from you a very fine smell.

He said: Yes, I have with me a mistress who is the most scented of the women of Arabia. He said: Allow me to smell (the scent on your head). He said: Yes, you may smell. So he caught it and smelt. Then he said: Allow me to do so (once again).

He then held his head fast and said to his companions: Do your job. And they killed him.

What does this story tell us? Muhammad wants to kill a Jew named Ka'B B. Ashraf. Why? Because he has insulted Allah and Muhammad. His "insults" were in the form of poetry. Ka'B was an accomplished poet. He wrote a poem lamenting the slaughter conducted by the Muslims at a battle.

63

Muhammad asks for volunteers to commit the murder. Playing upon a long friendship with the murder victim, the messenger of Allah's volunteer executioner (also named Muhammad) uses deception saying he wants to borrow money from the victim. Going to his house at night one man holds Ka'B's head while the others kill him.

Another Infidel is dead making Allah and his messenger very happy! If you are a Muslim child growing up learning these types of stories, how can you not be infected by the idea that Allah wants you to kill Jews and other non-Muslims for him.

As a child, I grew up hearing how the leader of my faith was loving and forgiving. That he loved everyone in the world regardless of race or faith. Jesus never commanded his followers to kill for him. In fact he prevented Peter from doing so telling him to "put away his sword."

I plead not guilty by reason of "MID"

These next two stories from the life of Muhammad illustrate the successful use of the Muhammad Insult Defense or "MID." Thanks to the not guilty by reason of "MID" defense, you do not even need a high priced defense attorney to get you acquitted. This defense allows you to represent yourself. Every time it is used it results in full acquittal from the crime of murder.

Muslim Hadith Book 38, Number 4348
Narrated by Abdullah Ibn Abbas

A blind man had a slave-mother who used to abuse the Prophet (peace be upon him) and disparage him. He forbade her but she did not stop. He rebuked her but she did not give up her habit. One night she began to slander the Prophet (peace be upon him) and abuse him.

So he took a dagger, placed it on her belly, pressed it, and killed her. A child who came between her legs was smeared with the blood that was there. When the morning came, the Prophet (peace be upon him) was informed about it.

He assembled the people and said: I adjure by Allah the man who has done this action and I adjure him by my right to him that he should stand up. Jumping over the necks of the people and trembling the man stood up.

He sat before the Prophet (peace be upon him) and said: Apostle of Allah! I am her master; she used to abuse you and disparage you. I forbade her, but she did not stop, and I rebuked her, but she did not abandon her habit. I have two sons like pearls from her, and she was my companion. Last night she began to abuse and disparage you. So I took a dagger, put it on her belly and pressed it till I killed her.

Thereupon the Prophet (peace be upon him) said: Oh be witness, no retaliation is payable for her blood.

Muslim Hadith Book 38, Number 4349
Narrated by Ali ibn AbuTalib

A Jewess used to abuse the Prophet (peace be upon him) and disparage him. A man strangled her till she died. The Apostle of Allah (peace be upon him) declared that no recompense was payable for her blood.

Clearly Muhammad approved of the killing of non-Muslims for insulting him and/or Allah. Islam believes itself to be so superior that it forces those outside the faith to bow to its demands even to the point of death. Think about this for a minute. To demand others to treat your faith in a way that you deem to be appropriate and kill them if they do not is arrogant.

To impose death on those who do not hold your beliefs and who "insult" your faith is evil. Modern Muslim's carry out

Muhammad's wishes even today. As an example, this from a story by Robert Spencer entitled, "Islam Insulted in Egypt: One Stabbed, Three Killed," dated October 27, 2005. The following is an excerpt from this piece, found at www.Humanevents.com.

The Muslim Brotherhood has threatened to kill Coptic Pope Shenouda III. A nun was stabbed by a Muslim who burst into a Coptic Church shouting "Allah akbar." Three people were killed as thousands of Muslim protestors rioted outside a Coptic church in Alexandria, Egypt. Relations between Muslims and Christians in Egypt have not been this tense in recent memory.

By all accounts, it's because of a DVD shown in a Coptic church that Muslims think insults Islam. How exactly? According to CNN, "The riot was sparked by the distribution of a DVD of a play that was performed at the church two years ago. The play, I Was Blind But Now I Can See, *tells the story of a young Christian who converts to Islam and becomes disillusioned.*

In the first chapter of this book, I discussed a 2006 protest in London by angry Muslims. Slogans on the protest signs were clear about their attitude towards "insulters of Islam." Their signs read "slay those who insult Islam," "butcher those who mock Islam," and "exterminate those who slander Islam." Where did these Muslims get the ideas for the slogans? I used to think that Muslims like this were false representatives of their faith. I believed these protestors were radical extremists that were not part of true Islam. But it turns out they are just doing what Muhammad asks them to do. These protestors are reflecting the true Islam as practiced by the most holy revered founder of their faith.

In 2006 Muslims around the world conducted violent protests over cartoons published that according to them "insulted"

Muhammad and Islam. Embassies were set on fire and several people were killed. It has been 1400 years after Muhammad died, and his calls for violence when he is "insulted" are still listened to and followed. This should not be ignored. Muhammad founded Islam and His followers are expected to pay close attention to what he taught through word and deed.

Kill those who commit adultery

During his ministry on earth, Jesus was given an opportunity to pass judgement on a woman who was caught in the act of adultery. Here is the story from the New Testament gospel of John.

✝

The teachers of the law and the Pharisees brought in a woman caught in adultery. They made her stand before the group and said to Jesus, "Teacher this women was caught in the act of adultery. In the law Moses commanded us to stone such women. Now what do you say?"

They were using this question as a trap, in order to have a basis for accusing him. But Jesus bent down and started to write on the ground with his finger. When they kept on questioning him, he straightened up and said to them, "If any one of you is without sin, let him be the first to throw a stone at her." Again he stooped down and wrote on the ground.

At this, those who heard began to go away one at a time, the older ones first, until only Jesus was left, with the woman still standing there. Jesus straightened up and asked her, "Woman, where are they? Has no one condemned you?" "No one, sir," she said. "Then neither do I condemn you," Jesus declared. "Go now and leave your life of sin."

John 8:3-11

Christians learn many lessons from this story. Jesus shows forgiveness, mercy, and how to be against sinful behavior but still value the person committing it. The idea Christ puts forth that only those without sin should cast the first stone is profound. All of us know that we have made mistakes and have done things that are against the laws of God. As the Bible says "all have sinned and fallen short of the Glory of God."

No one is able to cast the first stone because no one is without sin. Jesus ushered in a new era of forgiveness available to all. Adultery is still a sin, and Jesus tells the woman to "leave your life of sin." But Christ's forgiveness allows this woman to continue to live and have the opportunity to change her life for the good.

Everybody must be stoned

I know people who have once had moral problems but have, with the help of faith, turned their lives around. They have become positive influences for God, helping others who may be on the wrong path. Even though Christ's lesson had been around for 600 years for Muhammad to learn, he rejects it for his own teaching. Muhammad reinstates the death penalty for adultery which Christ had removed.

Muslim Hadith Book 38, Number 4421
Narrated by Al-Lajlaj al-Amiri

I was working in the market. A woman passed carrying a child. The people rushed towards her, and I also rushed along with them.

I then went to the Prophet (peace be upon him) while he was asking: Who is the father of this (child) who is with you? She remained silent.

A young man by her side said: I am his father, Apostle of Allah! He then turned towards her and asked: Who is the father of this child with you?

The young man said: I am his father, Apostle of Allah! The Apostle of Allah (peace be upon him) then looked at some of those who were around him and asked them about him. They said: We only know good (about him).

The Prophet (peace be upon him) said to him: Are you married? He said: Yes. So he gave orders regarding him and he was stoned to death.

He (the narrator) said: We took him out, dug a pit for him and put him in it. We then threw stones at him until he died.

Bukhari Hadith Volume 8, Book 82, Number 806
Narrated by AbuHuraira

A man came to Allah's Apostle while he was in the mosque, and he called him, saying, "O Allah's Apostle! I have committed illegal sexual intercourse." The Prophet turned his face to the other side, but that man repeated his statement four times, and after he bore witness against himself four times, the Prophet called him, saying, "Are you mad?" The man said, "No." The Prophet said, "Are you married?" The man said, "Yes." Then the Prophet said, "Take him away and stone him to death." Jabir bin Abdullah said: I was among the ones who participated in stoning him and we stoned him at the Musalla. When the stones troubled him, he fled, but we over took him at Al-Harra and stoned him to death.

In another version of the previous story the man tells the Muslims that he was tricked into admitting his sin to Muhammad. He thought that he would obtain mercy and forgiveness if he confessed his sin to the prophet. Instead he got a death sentence.

When he tried to escape they tracked him down and finished the job of killing him. Here are two other stoning stories.

Bukhari Hadith Volume 8, Book 82, Number 809
Narrated by Ibn 'Umar

A Jew and a Jewess were brought to Allah's Apostle on a charge of committing an illegal sexual intercourse. The Prophet asked them. "What is the legal punishment (for this sin) in your Book (Torah)?"

They replied, "Our priests have innovated the punishment of blackening the faces with charcoal and Tajbiya." 'Abdullah bin Salam said, "O Allah's Apostle, tell them to bring the Torah." The Torah was brought, and then one of the Jews put his hand over the Divine Verse of the Rajam (stoning to death) and started reading what preceded and what followed it.

On that, Ibn Salam said to the Jew, "Lift up your hand." Behold! The Divine Verse of the Rajam was under his hand. So Allah's Apostle ordered that the two (sinners) be stoned to death, and so they were stoned. Ibn 'Umar added: So both of them were stoned at the Balat, and I saw the Jew sheltering the Jewess.

Muslim Hadith Book 017, Number 4207

Imran b. Husain reported that a woman from Juhaina came to Allah's Apostle (may peace be upon him) and she had become pregnant because of adultery. She said: Allah's Apostle, I have done something for which (prescribed punishment) must be imposed upon me, so impose that. Allah's Apostle (may peace be upon him) called her master and said: Treat her well, and when she delivers bring her to me. He did accordingly.

Then Allah's Apostle (may peace be upon him) pronounced judgment about her and her clothes were tied around her and then he commanded and she was stoned to death. He then prayed over her (dead body). Thereupon Umar said to him: Allah's Apostle, you offer prayer for her, whereas she had committed adultery!

Thereupon he said: She has made such a repentance that if it were to be divided among seventy men of Medina, it would be enough. Have you found any repentance better than this that she sacrificed her life for Allah, the Majestic?

Do these stories bother you as they do me? Muhammad shows no mercy or forgiveness. Muhammad takes upon himself the power of death over Jews who do not follow Muslim law. In the story of the Jewish couple, the dying Jew shows more compassion and selflessness than his judge as he tries to shelter the Jewish women from the stones.

In the last story, Muhammad defines the "best repentance" as the "sacrifice" of the sinner's life for Allah. Repentance is a concept that means turning your life around. You are going along in your life doing something wrong. You then turn your life around by stopping the sinful activity and living a morally right life.

The Muslim concept that dying for Allah is a form of repentance, gives you no opportunity to turn your life around and live for God. It gives no chance to be an example to others of the positive change that can be made in a life that is dedicated to serve God.

In the theology of the Christian faith, God sends his only Son to die for the sins of the world. This allows us to obtain forgiveness of sin and not suffer the punishment that we deserve. Christ pays the debt for our sin and takes the punishment.

Stoning still practiced by modern Muslims

Stoning is still practiced by some of Islam's faithful in modern times. John David Powell illustrates this in his story about a modern stoning that took place in Iran. The story, found at www.therealitycheck.org, is entitled "They Still Are Not Like Us: New stoning video cause to revisit past." The video shows that 1400 years later the execution commands as instituted by the Apostle of Allah are followed with precision.

Rep. Gary Ackerman, D-NY, showed a smuggled video of a public stoning in Iran. Online at www.apostatesofislam.com/media/stoning.htm, is a copy of the 15-minute tape. It is a gruesome account, and should not be viewed by the merely curious or those easily sickened by terrifying images of torture.

About five minutes into the tape we see a group of men carrying an individual in a sheet to the center of the plaza, and we watch as they transform the sheet into a death shroud. They carefully place the mummy-like figure into a hole as if transplanting a tree in someone's yard.

At about seven minutes into the tape, handlers place a second person into another hole. This raw video shows us the backs of people as the photographer walks around looking for a clear view of the gruesome scene of death. About 30 seconds later, hundreds of men, mostly members of Iran's Revolutionary Guard, crowd into a circle around the condemned.

Then the stoning begins, seemingly spontaneously. We watch the eerie site of two white figures writhing as stones hit them. A man walks up to one shroud and pelts it with rocks. The camera zooms in on the bloodied lump surrounded by stones. The camera pans to the other individual. The cover is knocked off, he is face down, his head is bathed in blood.

The tape jumps to the scene of a third person brought in, shrouded. He stands stock still as ghastly gardeners plant him in the hole.

Dirt is shoveled into the hole around the fourth individual, who bends at the waist. Feet tamp the dirt around him, making sure all is snug.

The circle of death reforms as the man with the shovel makes his final tamps. The crowd chants in agitated anticipation.

The stoning begins with lusty yells. It is a frenzied scene devoid of humanity. Scores of stones fly quickly and strike horribly. The shroud around one head explodes into red. The two ghostly figures totter. One falls forward only to be pelted backward. The camera zooms in.

The man on the right writhes as his shroud comes loose. We see his bloody torso struck by stones. We see him struggle as the pile of stones grows around him. We see the circle contract slowly until fewer than five feet separate the murderous men from the objects of their execution. Stone throwers stand close enough to caress their victims. But they do not. Instead, they pick up more stones and fling them with all their might.

The condemned continue to writhe, to fall over, to sit back up, to fall back over. One goes suddenly still. The other rises, almost defiantly in the face of a hard death.

Now the crowd stands within inches. Men pick up rocks as quickly as they can, in some macabre competition to see who will cast the last stone in the deliverance of Allah's justice.

As I viewed the stoning video, I felt like I was not in modern times. It was as if I had been transported back to a primitive brutal time. Think about it for a minute. Could you pick up rocks and hurl them at another human being for 30 minutes or so until they bleed out and die? There is probably not one person reading this who could. But if you were a sincere follower of Muhammad and Allah you could be required to do so.

It is possible that some would even experience pleasure in the fulfillment of their "religious duty." It shows in the video. Perhaps these Muslims feel a rush of "god like" power, as they become the hands of justice for Allah the "compassionate, the merciful." It is unknown for what offense the men were being executed.

It is certain that executions for adultery do take place in the Muslim world today. In 2007, Iran stoned a man convicted of adultery. This was detailed in a July 10, 2007 article entitled "UN Rights Chief Condemns Stoning Execution of Iranian Convicted of Adultery" found at www.jurist.law.pitt.edu.

According to the article the man had been in prison for more than eleven years. In 2002 Iran had issued a moratorium on stoning executions. Iran is also a party to the International Covenant on Civil and Political Rights. Countries who sign this treaty are agreeing to impose the death penalty only for serious violent crimes. However, in spite of moratorium and the international treaty, the stoning was carried out.

Within the Iranian parliament, reform minded members have sought to outlaw the stoning of convicted adulterers. However, their efforts have been thwarted by clerics who take the injunctions in the Koran and the actions of Muhammad seriously in regards to stoning.

Teenage girl stoned in Turkey

This next story is from a woman in Turkey who had a sister that was stoned by men in her village for committing what they said was adultery. Islam, when truly followed, produces results like this. In this case the government was not involved. Instead, family and religious leaders were the hands of Allah's justice.

This story entitled "An Untold Love Story" can be found at www.faithfreedom.org.

An Untold Love Story
By Yagmur Dursun
2005/03/13

My name is Yagmur (it means "rain"). I was born in rural Turkey, in a village. Generally Turkish women enjoy many freedoms, which our Arab sisters can't even think of. Rural Turkey is a different story. Honour killings take place every day, women don't have much say (if any) in household matters and female employment is out of question. However, much hard work is done by women because men don't want to strain themselves; women are like cattle or slaves. If a husband tells you to do something, you have to obey.

My mother was a fairly educated woman, she taught me at home and I even went to school. My hobby was reading books. Through them I learnt different languages and acquired a lot of knowledge. I was a disciplined and obedient girl, unlike my sister who was somewhat uppity.

When she was 18, she fell in love with a young man. They both loved each other, but he was meant for another girl, thus his parents had decided. Dating is utterly forbidden in Islam, marriages are arranged and often young people meet on their wedding day.

My sister was rebellious. She "dated" that young man. Every night she would go to see him. They even kissed and actually their relationship went too far. She got pregnant. At first they planned to run away to a big city where they would be safe. They knew in villages, religion rules and they could be in trouble. Authorities don't care what's going on in rural Turkey. Sometimes imams, mullahs and elders who try to practice Sharia and break the secular state law are punished but usually authorities are more interested in big cities full of tourists and turn a blind eye to what happens in villages.

I remember their young faces. I didn't understand the whole situation; I was a little girl. But when I looked at them I could see they were happy. Their happiness made me happy too and I wanted to smile. Instead of eloping, they decided to speak to my father. "Pregnancy is a very good reason to get permission for marriage," or so they thought.

Alas, my sister had miscalculated my father's love for her and his obsession with his religion. He became furious. Instead of letting the two young lovers marry and build their nest of love, he took her to the religious elders and they ruled that she had committed adultery. She was sentenced to death by stoning. They showed no mercy even for her unborn child.

She had stained the "honor" of the family and the only way to remove that stain was to nip her life in the bud. Her unborn baby was a stain too, and that little creature had to be destroyed as well, so my family could live honorably.

In the evening before her execution, she came to my room and told me that she would miss me. She was crying and hugged me to her bosom. Then she smiled and said that soon she would see her unborn baby. I was blissfully unaware of her fate, but I felt that something bad was about to happen. I was so scared!

I still remember her black eyes; she stared at the sky while she was dug into the ground. She was wrapped in white sheets and her hands were tied to her body. She was buried up to her waist. The rabid mob circled her with stones in their hands and started throwing them at her while the roars of Allah-u-Akbar Allah-u-Akbar added to their frenzy. She twitched with pain as the stones hit her tender body and smashed her head. Blood gushed out from her face, cheeks, mouth, nose and eyes. All she could do was to bend to the left and to the right. Gradually the movements slowed down and finally she stopped moving even though the shower of the stones did not stop. Her head fell on her chest. Her bloodied face remained serene. All the pain had gone.

The hysteric mob relented and the chant of Allah-u' Akbar stopped. Someone approached and with a big boulder in his hand smashed the scull of my sister to finish her off. There was no need for that; she was already dead. Her bright black eyes that beamed with life were shut. Her jovial laughter that filled the world around her was silenced. Her heart that beat with such a heavenly love for only a short time had stopped.

Her unborn baby was not given a chance to breathe one breath of air. He (or she) accompanied his young mother in her solitary and cold tomb, or who knows, maybe to a better place where love reigns and pain and ignorance are not known. These two budding lives had to be nipped so my father could keep his honor.

But the saddest part is that according to Islam my sister deserved that death. The elders were sure she would be burning in Hell for eternity. No, I can't imagine that God can send someone to Hell for loving and for being happy. I can't accept a cruel God.

www.faithfreedom.org/testimonials/yagmur50313.htm

Yagmur's story is powerful in many ways. Islam's religious goal seems to be to destroy not save. There is no second chance offered. Those who condemned this girl did not do so without justification. The village religious elders simply copied the actions of the prophet who had himself condemned girls to death.

Kill those who believe in many gods

These next Hadith stories discuss the killing of those who believe there are many gods (polytheists). The Apostle of Allah himself gave his followers the commands to kill.

Muslim Hadith Book 14, Number 2632
Narrated by Salamah ibn al-Akwa'

The Apostle of Allah (peace be upon him) appointed AbuBakr our commander and we fought with some people who were polytheists, and we attacked them at night, killing them. Our war-cry that night was "put to death; put to death." Salamah said: I killed that night with my hand polytheists belonging to seven houses.

Muslim Hadith Book 14, Number 2664
Narrated by Samurah ibn Jundub

The Prophet (peace be upon him) said: Kill the old men who are polytheists, but spare their children.

If you think you are safe because you are not a "polytheist," remember that the Koran teaches that Christians believe and worship "many gods." This is because Christianity teaches that God is a trinity composed of The Father, Son and Holy Spirit. Therefore Christians are, by Muslim reckoning, "polytheists."

In 2004 Nick Berg was murdered by Muslims in Iraq. Before they slowly and painfully sawed his head off they read a statement. Dave Huntwork, in a May 23, 2004 piece entitled "The Nature Of The Enemy," found at www.newswithviews.com, gives us an English translation of the statement. How do you think these Muslims interpret the Holy Writings of Islam's commands regarding polytheists?

The praise of Allah for all Muslims with his support and the humiliating of those who attempt to defeat Islam and who attack it and who entice the unbelievers with their cunning... He has ordered the prophet — peace be upon him — and he is master the merciful one, with the slitting of the necks of some prisoners and their slow killing.

And for us it is an example and a good example... we tell you to know that the coffins will arrive to you one coffin after another, as your people are slaughtered in this way... Then you kill the polytheists (Christians) where you find them and you take them and count them and place them where they can be seen... Allah is the greatest and the honor to Allah and to its messenger and to the militants.

And our last claim is that the praise of Allah is the Lord of the Worlds.... And you see the slaughter your fighting brothers suspend the head of this unbeliever on one of Baghdad bridges so that they teach a lesson to others from the infidels and serves as a witness to the honor of the Muslims.

There are still a sizeable number of people in our world today who believe in many gods. If Christians are counted among them due to their belief in the trinity, then more than one half of the population are "polytheists" according to Islam. The Jewish faith worships one God so maybe they are safe. Or maybe not, as you will see in these next verses.

Kill non-Muslims for Allah

The following quotes from both the Koran and Muhammad's sayings give a series of commands that make it clear that Allah and his messenger desire that non-Muslims be fought until everyone is Muslim. Muslims who take these verses at face value are justified by their faith in committing any act of violence or terrorism against any non-Muslim.

"Fight then against them (non-Muslims) till strife be at an end, and the religion be all of it Allah's."
The Koran, Chapter 8:40

This verse reminds me of a passage in the New Testament that says "every knee shall bow and every tongue confess that Jesus Christ is Lord." The passage speaks of a time to come when all people will acknowledge that Christ is the Lord (ruler) over all. People will bow (show him respect and submission) whether they want to or not.

At this time, Christianity will be the only religion. This thought may disturb those who do not believe in Christ. However there is a major difference between this Christian concept of the supremacy of Christ and the Islamic doctrine of the supremacy of Allah and his messenger.

Islam commands its followers to use violence to make Allah Lord of all, here and now on the earth. The supremacy of Christ happens by the power of God. The idea of using violence to bring your beliefs to the world is dangerous. What if you are mistaken? What if your beliefs are wrong?

The apostle Paul experienced this. He traveled to various cities using violence on Christians to try and stamp out the faith. Then, according to the New Testament, Christ gave him a vision that his beliefs were wrong. After this encounter with Jesus on the road to Damascus, Paul became a follower of the same faith he used to persecute. He went on to be a leader in the Christian movement and wrote many of the books in the Bible.

In his new role as leader in the Christian Faith, Paul did not use any force or violence. Paul was sincere when he persecuted Christians. He honestly believed he was doing what God wanted him to do. But Paul was wrong. Sincerity of belief does not make you right. Strongly held convictions do not cause violence. Moving from personal conviction to imposing your beliefs on others does.

Make war not love

Make war upon such of those to whom the Scriptures have been given as believe not in Allah, or in the Last Day, and who forbid not that which Allah and His Apostle have forbidden, and who profess not the profession of truth, until they pay tribute out of hand, and they be humbled.
The Koran, Chapter 9:29

Believers! wage war against such of the infidels as are your neighbors, and let them find you rigorous: and know that Allah is with those who fear him.
The Koran, Chapter 9:123

O Prophet! Make war on the infidels and hypocrites, and deal rigorously with them. **The Koran, Chapter 66:9**

Remember, the Koran is the message of Allah to the world. In these verses, Allah is commanding his followers to make war on anyone who believes differently. If you do not believe in Allah, and you do not live your life as Muhammad did, then you are fair game to be killed or become a second class citizen (be humbled).

Those who want to excuse the violent nature of Islam try and interpret these verses symbolically. They say that these passages are speaking of war as a metaphor of the struggle to submit to Allah. By looking at Muhammad's life one should be able to answer the question of interpretation. Did Muhammad interpret these verses as a symbolic metaphor or literally? The next passages show actual examples from his life.

Bukhari Hadith Volume 4, Book 52, Number 50
Narrated by Anas bin Malik

The Prophet said, "A single endeavor (of fighting) in Allah's Cause in the forenoon or in the afternoon is better than the world and whatever is in it."

Bukhari Hadith Volume 4, Book 52, Number 176
Narrated by 'Abdullah bin 'Ulmar

Allah's Apostle said, "You (i.e. Muslims) will fight with the Jews till some of them will hide behind stones. The stones will (betray them) saying, 'O 'Abdullah (i.e. slave of Allah)! There is a Jew hiding behind me; so kill him.' "

Bukhari Hadith Volume 8, Book 82, Number 795
Narrated by Anas

The Prophet cut off the hands and feet of the men belonging to the tribe of 'Uraina and did not cauterise (their bleeding limbs) till they died.

Bukhari Hadith Volume 9, Book 84, Number 64
Narrated by 'Ali

No doubt I heard Allah's Apostle saying, "During the last days there will appear some young foolish people who will say the best words, but their faith will not go beyond their throats (i.e. they will have no faith) and will go out from (leave) their religion as an arrow goes out of the game. So, where-ever you find them, kill them, for who-ever kills them shall have reward on the Day of Resurrection."

Muhammad clearly acted on the Koran verses by taking them literally. There is nothing symbolic about the fighting and killing commanded and done by Allah's messenger. The quote at the beginning of this chapter also illustrates this point well.

Modern day Muslims make Holy War

Modern day Muslims in the Sudan take these passages at face value. For decades they have been making war on infidels in the Sudan with the goal that "the religion be all of it Allah's." Sabit A. Alley discusses this in his piece entitled "War and Genocide in the Sudan" found at www.iabolish.org.

For over four decades now the Sudan has been engulfed in a bitter and devastating civil war between its Northern and Southern regions. The causes of the war are varied and complex, but generally they hinge on the North's hegemonic designs over the people of the South.

Since independence on January 1, 1956 successive Arab and Muslim dominated governments in Khartoum have strived to forcefully bring the South under the Arab and Islamic fold. These governments, and especially the current National Islamic Fundamentalist government, have used and continue to use war methods or weapons such as slavery, Arabization, Islamization, ethnic cleansing, aerial bombardment and man-made famine to either decimate or subjugate the African people of the Southern Sudan and Nuba Mountains.

The National Islamic government has even gone as far as to declare "Jihad," an Islamic Holy war against the people of the South and the Nuba Mountains, who it considers as infidels and who must be totally eradicated or brought under the banner of Arabism and Islamism.

Are you as shocked as I am at the thirst for blood displayed by Allah and his prophet? If you are a man or women of good will how can you not be. The prophet commands his followers to "fight with all men" until they become Muslim or are ruled over by Islam. All men are to agree that there is no God but Allah and that Muhammad is his messenger. Furthermore, all must pray in the direction of Mecca, eat the same food, and pray like Muslims. Those who will not cooperate are to be killed or enslaved.

Christ never commanded any armies to go and kill his enemies. In fact Jesus commanded his followers to show kindness and compassion to their enemies. Christ even tells his followers to pray for their enemies. Christ's words can be hard to live by because they are against our natural tendencies to fight those with whom we disagree.

Muhammad's commands are in a way easier to follow because they match up with some of the natural tendencies in human nature. Many people want to be part of a big cause. They want to believe that God is on their side. There are those who like to be right and let others know it. Most stop short of murder because they know that it is wrong, or they just can't bring themselves to do it.

But what if the highest spiritual leader of a faith encouraged his followers to kill for God? Many followers would answer the call to kill. This is exactly how it plays out time and time again in the Islamic community.

Bin Laden directs followers to kill

Osama Bin Laden uses the Koran and Hadith to encourage Muslims to kill. From various accounts by those who know him, Osama is a very devout Muslim. Before the invasion of Iraq, Bin Laden gave his directions to the faithful. He quotes some of the same passages that we have reviewed in this chapter. Here is a sampling of his February 12, 2003 audio message found at www.news.bbc.co.uk.

In the name of Allah, the merciful, the compassionate. A message to our Muslim brothers in Iraq, may God's peace, mercy, and blessings be upon you.

O you who believe fear Allah, by doing all that He has ordered and by abstaining from all that He has forbidden as He should be feared. Obey Him, be thankful to Him, and remember Him always, and die not except in a state of Islam [as Muslims] with complete submission to Allah.

Prophet Muhammad, Allah's peace be upon him, said: "Avoid the seven grave sins; polytheism, sorcery, killing, unless permitted by Allah, usury, taking the money of orphans, fleeing from combat, and slandering innocent faithful women."

Also, all grave sins, such as consuming alcohol, committing adultery, disobeying parents, and committing perjury. We must obey Allah in general, and should in particular mention the name of Allah more before combat.

We stress the importance of the martyrdom operations against the enemy — operations that inflicted harm on the United States and Israel that have been unprecedented in their history, thanks to Almighty Allah.

We also point out that whoever supported the United States, including the hypocrites of Iraq or the rulers of Arab countries, those who approved their actions and followed them in this crusade war by fighting with them or providing bases and administrative support, or any form of support, even by words, to kill the Muslims in Iraq, should know that they are apostates and outside the community of Muslims.

It is permissible to spill their blood and take their property.

Allah says: "O ye who believe! Take not the Jews and the Christians for your friends and protectors: they are but friends and protectors to each other." And he amongst you that turns to them [for friendship] is of them. Verily, Allah guideth not an unjust people.

We also stress to honest Muslims that they should move, incite, and mobilize the [Islamic] nation, amid such grave events and hot atmosphere so as to liberate themselves from those unjust and renegade ruling regimes, which are enslaved by the United States. They should also do so to establish the rule of Allah on earth.
www.news.bbc.co.uk/1/hi/world/middle_east/2751019.stm

As I said in previous chapters, before I read the Koran I thought that Bin Laden was twisting and distorting Islam to motivate Muslims to fight in his cause. But now, when I look at his words, I see that he is quoting the verses as the Koran gives them. Osama is learned in the Holy Writings of Islam. He knows what Muhammad said and applies it to our time. Bin Laden takes the words of Allah at face value and interprets it literally.

Vengeance is yours says Allah

What caught my eye in this next verse of the Koran is the idea that Allah is commanding his followers to take vengeance on infidels (non-Muslims). The passage indicates Allah could take vengeance on them himself, but instead, wants Muslims to prove their faith by doing Allah's work of revenge for him.

When ye encounter the infidels, strike off their heads till ye have made a great slaughter among them, and of the rest make fast the fetters. And afterwards let there either be free dismissals or ransomings, till the war hath laid down its burdens. Thus do. Were such the pleasure of Allah, He could

Himself take vengeance upon them: but He would rather prove the one of you by the other.

And whoso fight for the cause of Allah, their words He will not suffer to miscarry; He will vouchsafe them guidance, and dispose their hearts aright; And He will bring them into Paradise, of which He hath told them. Believers! if ye help Allah, Allah will help you, and will set your feet firm: But as for the infidels, let them perish: and their works shall Allah bring to nought. **The Koran, Chapter 47:4-9**

The Bible teaches a completely different message. This is at the core of living at peace with others who are different than you in faith. In Christianity it is God who takes vengeance. It is for God to decide how to judge humans. As humans we make mistakes. We cannot judge with complete unbiased fairness and correctness. God can and will. That is why we leave the vengeance up to the Perfect Judge who can apply it rightly.

Do not take revenge, my friends, but leave room for God's wrath, for it is written: "It is mine to avenge; I will repay," says the Lord. **Romans 12:19**

For we know him who said, "It is mine to avenge; I will repay," and again, "The Lord will judge his people." **Hebrews 10:30**

Allah loves a cheerful killer

Commands to kill for Allah are certainly a part of the Muslim faith. They are in the Koran and are found in the words and actions of the founder of Islam. Death is prescribed for insulting

Muhammad and/or Allah. Adulterers must be stoned. Anyone who believes in other gods besides Allah must die. Unless you pray like the Muslims and eat what they do, you must be killed or enslaved. Better not touch anything that Muhammad forbids or else you will be punished. Jews must die. Polytheists must die. Christians must die. Non-Muslims must die. Homosexuals must die. On and on the thirst for blood goes.

As noted before, as of May 2008, Muslims have carried out 11,098 attacks since 9/11. Is it undeniable that the Koranic verses and the example that Muhammad set are the inspiration for this violence.

The killing of another human being is the highest form of violence. Life is precious and once gone cannot be recovered. These verses raise killing to a high form of religious duty.

As I demonstrated in the previous chapter, Islam instills in the hearts and minds of believers an attitude of hate and contempt for non-Muslims. This helps to pave the way for acceptance of the commands to kill. That which is hateful and contemptible is worthless and should be destroyed. Allah truly loves a cheerful killer.

Unbelievers Turn or Burn

> *"Come now, let us reason together,"* says the LORD.
> *"Though your sins are like scarlet,*
> *they shall be as white as snow;*
> *though they are red as crimson,*
> *they shall be like wool."*
>
> God

> *Fight then against them till strife be at an end,*
> *and the religion be all of it Allah's.*
>
> Allah

The third major element of Islam that causes acts of violence like 9/11 are the commands to force Islamic beliefs on non-Muslims. Those who refuse to convert to Islam are to be killed or at best become second class citizens of the Islamic Republic. The Koran teaches this, and Muhammad in his words and actions lived it. Some Muslims will point to the following verses of the Koran to argue that force is not a part of Islam.

Say: O ye unbelievers! I worship not that which ye worship, and ye do not worship that which I worship; I shall never worship that which ye worship, neither will ye worship that which I worship. To you be your religion; and to me my religion. **The Koran, Chapter 109:1**

Let there be no compulsion in religion.
The Koran, Chapter 2:256

The problem is there are other verses that contradict these with commands to use force on unbelievers. I have already discussed the bi-polar nature of the Koran and Hadith in my "Islam 101" chapter. It is the belief of many Muslims that these non-force verses have been canceled and replaced by the violent verses.

Certainly the actions of Muhammad followed the idea of "unbelievers turn or burn" rather than the concept of "let there be no compulsion in religion."

Jews turn or burn

Muslim Hadith Book 019, Number 4363

It has been narrated on the authority of Abu Huraira who said: We were (sitting) in the mosque when the Messenger of Allah (may peace be upon him) came to us and said: (Let us) go to the Jews. We went out with him until we came to them. The Messenger of Allah (may peace be upon him) stood up and called out to them (saying): O ye assembly of Jews, accept Islam (and) you will be safe.

They said: Abu'l-Qasim, you have communicated (God's Message to us). The Messenger of Allah (may peace be upon him) said: I want this (i.e. you should admit that God's Message has been communicated to you), accept Islam and you would be safe.

They said: Abu'l-Qisim, you have communicated (Allah's Message). The Messenger of Allah (may peace be upon him) said: I want this... He said to them (the same words) the third time (and on getting the same reply) he added: You should know that the earth belongs to Allah and His Apostle, and I wish that I should expel you from this land. Those of you who have any property with them should sell it, otherwise they should know that the earth belongs to Allah and His Apostle (and they may have to go away leaving everything behind).

In this story Muhammad goes to a group of people from another faith and tells them that they must give up their faith and convert to his faith. The Jews are told that they will be "safe" if they become Muslims. Otherwise they must sell their property and be expelled from their land. Muhammad does not show a desire to live side by side with other faiths. He wants to force his views on others by the use of threats and violence.

The early Christians went to people of other faiths also. But they preached God's word without threats of force, violence or ultimatums. The Christian faith was spread by words not swords. Here is a description of two of the early Christians and how they spoke with those of other faiths. The passage credits the effective explanation of the Christian message for the results of people converting to the Christian Faith.

✠

At Iconium Paul and Barnabas went as usual into the Jewish Synagogue. There they spoke so effectively that a great number of Jews and Gentiles believed. **Acts 14:1**

Like Muhammad, Paul and Barnabas went to the Jews. But unlike Muhammad, Paul and Barnabas used reason and persuasion instead of threats to gain acceptance of their message.

The next story shows the messenger of Allah making good on his promise to expel Jews. I do not understand how anyone can put their faith in a man who did such things. Hitler is a symbol of evil because he exterminated millions. He expelled Jews from Germany, killed them and took their property. Maybe he was just following the example of Muhammad.

Muslim Hadith Book 019, Number 4364

It has been narrated on the authority of Ibn Umar that the Jews of Banu Nadir and Banu Quraizi fought against the Messenger of Allah (may peace be upon him) who expelled Banu Nadir, and allowed Quraiza to stay on, and granted favor to them until they too fought against him. Then he killed their men, and distributed their women, children and properties among the Muslims, except that some of them had joined the Messenger of Allah (may peace be upon him) who granted them security. They embraced Islam.

The Messenger of Allah (may peace be upon him) turned out all the Jews of Medina. Banu Cannaceae' (the tribe of 'Abdullah b. Salim) and the Jews of Banu Haritha and every other Jew who was in Medina.

Muhammad's approach to the Jews is to make a threat of death and slavery unless you accept Islam. There is no use of persuasion or reason. The prophet does not preach the word of Allah and give reasons for its truth. The Apostle of Allah does not allow a hearer of his message to consider the truth of it. The prophet just says here it is, take it or die. If you accept Islam, your wife, children and property are safe. If you fight against Islam, you will be killed and your wife, children and property will be given to Muslims.

God wants us to use our minds

Christianity has a much more intellectual approach. The God of the Bible says, "come let us reason together." Christ commanded his followers to preach the gospel (good news) to the entire world. But those who hear the preaching can decide for themselves. God's spirit is said to be working in the lives and hearts of those who hear the gospel. This is described as a "still small voice" working to convince people of the truth of the claims of Christ.

The Bible is full of history, prophecy and logical arguments for the faith. God gave us minds. It is not wrong for us to use them to examine the claims of someone who says they are speaking for God. In fact, it would be foolish to simply follow someone who claims to have a message from God without putting what they say to the test. Islam does not allow itself to be put to any test. Muhammad does not allow anyone to question his authority.

History is full of examples of people unquestioningly following false prophets who claimed to have a message from God. Blindly following a self-proclaimed prophet can lead to a bad ending. Jim Jones was a prophet who led hundreds of his followers to death in a mass murder and suicide in 1978.

More recently, in 1997, 38 members of the Heavens Gate group killed themselves at the direction of their prophet. They were told a spaceship that was riding on the Hale-Bopp comet was waiting to take their souls away.

The following verses out of the Bible show examples of believers using reason and thought to persuade others to the faith. Other Biblical passages give warnings to be careful about "false prophets."

✝

Taste and see that the LORD is good; blessed is the man who takes refuge in him.   **Psalm 34:7-9**

The 9/11 Verses

Now the Bereans were of more noble character than the Thessalonians, for they received the message with great eagerness and examined the Scriptures every day to see if what Paul said was true.   **Acts 17:10-12**

Here I am! I stand at the door and knock. If anyone hears my voice and opens the door, I will come in and eat with him, and he with me.   **Revelation 3:19-21**

After this, Paul left Athens and went to Corinth. There he met a Jew named Aquila, a native of Pontus, who had recently come from Italy with his wife Priscilla, because Claudius had ordered all the Jews to leave Rome. Paul went to see them, and because he was a tentmaker as they were, he stayed and worked with them. Every Sabbath he reasoned in the synagogue, trying to persuade Jews and Greeks.   **Acts 18:1-4**

Then Agrippa said to Paul, "Do you think that in such a short time you can persuade me to be a Christian?" Paul replied, "Short time or long—I pray God that not only you but all who are listening to me today may become what I am, except for these chains."   **Acts 26:28-29**

But in your hearts set apart Christ as Lord. Always be prepared to give an answer to everyone who asks you to give the reason for the hope that you have. But do this with gentleness and respect, keeping a clear conscience, so that those who speak maliciously against your good behavior in Christ may be ashamed of their slander.   **1 Peter 3:15-16**

In the presence of God and of Christ Jesus, who will judge the living and the dead, and in view of his appearing and his kingdom, I give you this charge: Preach the Word; be prepared in season and out of season; correct, rebuke and encourage—with great patience and careful instruction.   **2 Timothy 4:1-2**

Dear Friends, do not believe every spirit, but test the spirits to see whether they are from God, because many false prophets have gone out into the world. **1 John 4:1**

Watch out for false prophets. They come to you in sheep's clothing, but inwardly they are ferocious wolves. By their fruit you will recognize them. Do people pick grapes from thornbushes, or figs from thistles? Likewise every good tree bears good fruit, but a bad tree bears bad fruit. A good tree cannot bear bad fruit, and a bad tree cannot bear good fruit. Every tree that does not bear good fruit is cut down and thrown into the fire. Thus, by their fruit you will recognize them. **Matthew 7:15-20**

These verses from the Bible show that God wants people to use their minds to examine the claims of those who say that they speak for him. The early Christians are told to share their faith with unbelievers with "gentleness and respect." Paul preached every Sabbath trying to reason with and persuade the unbelievers. There is no force used.

The message is preached and it is up to the hearer to decide to accept it or not. Unlike Islam the receiver of the message of Christ is allowed to consider the claims for himself.

All unbelievers turn or burn

These next words and actions of the prophet expand his forced conversion activities beyond the Jews to all unbelievers.

Bukhari Hadith Volume 4, Book 52, Number 196
Narrated by Abu Huraira

Allah's Apostle said, "I have been ordered to fight with the people till they say, 'None has the right to be worshiped but

Allah,' and whoever says, 'None has the right to be worshiped but Allah,' his life and property will be saved by me except for Islamic law, and his accounts will be with Allah, (either to punish him or to forgive him)."

As I read this passage, I pictured people like you and me, who are practicing Jewish and Christian faiths as their forefathers have done for hundreds and thousands of years. Life is good and at peace.

Then along comes Muhammad with his threats. The men of the town meet together to decide what to do. Some organize armies and fight the Muslims. If they lose, their wives and children become the property of Muslim men. Their children are forced to become Muslims. Their wives become sexual property to be raped anytime their owners want them. The men are not around to see it all since they have been killed.

Some give up their faith and convictions to save their lives. Others flee, leaving houses and farms behind, which were built with generations of effort. In all this there is no thought, study or examining the truth of the claims of the prophet. There is only violent force. This lesson of force from the messenger of Allah has been imitated by Muslims over the centuries and is still happening today. Here is an example in a news story by Art Moore entitled "Sudan Jihad Forcing Islam on Christians, Using Rape and Killing" found at www.WorldNetDaily.com.

Posted: March 4, 2002
1:00 a.m. Eastern
By Art Moore
© 2002 www.WorldNetDaily.com
Sudan's militant Muslim regime is slaughtering Christians who refuse to convert to Islam, according to the head of an aid group who recently returned from the African nation. The

forced conversions are just one aspect of the Khartoum government's self-declared jihad on the mostly Christian and animist south, Dennis Bennett, executive director of Seattle-based Servant's Heart told WorldNetDaily.

Villagers in several areas of the northeast Upper Nile region say that when women are captured by government forces they are asked: "Are you Christian or Muslim?" Women who answer "Muslim" are set free, but typically soldiers gang rape those who answer "Christian" then cut off their breasts and leave them to die as an example for others.

Bennett says these stories are corroborated by witnesses from several tribes in the region. Upon returning to the U.S., he wrote a letter to influential members of Congress and activists.

"After witnessing once again the situation on the ground there," Bennett wrote, "I must ask 'How long will the United States government allow the Government of Sudan to continue its jihad against the Black African Christians of South Sudan?' "

Backed by Muslim clerics, the National Islamic Front regime in the Arab and Muslim north declared a jihad, or holy war, on the south in 1989. Since 1983, an estimated 2 million people have died from war and related famine. About 4.5 million have become refugees.

Sudan's holy war against the south was reaffirmed in October by First Vice President Ali Osman Taha. "The jihad is our way, and we will not abandon it and will keep its banner high," he said to a brigade of mujahedin fighters heading for the war front, according to Sudan's official SUNA news agency. "We will never sell out our faith and will never betray the oath to our martyrs."

The U.S. House of Representatives adopted a resolution finding that Khartoum is "systematically committing genocide," but current legislation that would impose sanctions has been stalled. The Sudan Peace Act is opposed by both the White House and Wall Street. Sanctions in the House version of the bill target oil revenues that Khartoum is using to fuel its war effort. Bennett, with 20 years experience in international risk management and banking, said he was the first to probe the link between oil and jihad that is now documented and publicized by human rights groups. His research began in 1996 when he asked: If you're the government of Sudan and you're broke, how are you paying for your war?

In his letter urging action by the U.S., he points out that Sudan's military continues to decorate and promote known war criminals such as Commander Taib Musba, who in the mid-1980s killed an estimated 15,000 unarmed, civilian, ethnic Uduk Christians. In 1986, Musba entered the Uduk tribal capital of Chali and declared to its Christians: "You are all going to convert from Christianity to Islam today, because here is what's going to happen to you if you don't."

Musba then killed five church leaders in front of the gathered villagers. When they refused to convert, he began killing unarmed men, women and children. Some were herded at gunpoint into a hut then run over by a 50-ton, Soviet-made tank. He also herded groups of about a dozen people into a hut, where he asked the first person "Do you renounce Jesus Christ?" Anyone who refused was killed by a three-inch nail driven into the top of the head.

Koran verses support forced conversions

The Koran has verses that support Muhammad's words and actions in the use of violence against unbelievers to force then to convert or be subject to Islam.

...kill those who join other gods with Allah (polytheist Arabs) wherever ye shall find them; and seize them; besiege them, and lay wait for them with every kind of ambush: but if they shall convert, and observe prayer, and pay the obligatory alms, then let them go their way, for Allah is gracious, merciful.

The Koran, Chapter 9:4

When the help of Allah and the victory arrive, and thou seest men entering the religion of Allah by troops; then utter the praise of thy Lord... The Koran, Chapter 110:1

Forced Conversions are a part of Islam

Any Muslim wishing to try and force conversions has plenty of Islamic texts to back up his actions. The scripture of Islam is where the idea of forcing people into the faith comes from in the first place. I disagree with those who would say the motivation for these killings is more political and ethnic than religious. The demands to convert to Islam and the promises of safety or death are evidence that Sudan Muslims are following the pattern set down by Muhammad.

The commands to force conversions are unique to the Islamic faith. Try doing a search on "forced conversion" on the Internet. You will find many references. Every one of them will be about Muslims trying to force conversions to Islam.

"Holy War" means holy war

The following words from Muhammad are the military orders to the commanders of the forces sent to fight the Holy War (jihad) for Allah. Muslims trying to downplay the violence that is a deep part of Islam will try to change the meaning of Jihad.

The 9/11 Verses

In the book, *The Everything® Understanding Islam Book*, by Christine Huda Dodge, jihad is defined as "The struggle to defend one's faith in the face of opposition." Clearly the prophet viewed a holy war (jihad) as an actual war using lethal force to make others conform to the will of Allah. This is an offensive not defensive action.

Muslim Hadith Book 019, Number 4294

It has been reported from Sulaiman b. Buraid through his father that when the Messenger of Allah (may peace be upon him) appointed anyone as leader of an army or detachment he would especially exhort him to fear Allah and to be good to the Muslims who were with him.

He would say: Fight in the name of Allah and in the way of Allah. Fight against those who disbelieve in Allah. Make a holy war, do not embezzle the spoils; do not break your pledge; and do not mutilate (the dead) bodies; do not kill the children.

When you meet your enemies who are polytheists, invite them to three courses of action. If they respond to any one of these, you also accept it and withhold yourself from doing them any harm. Invite them to (accept) Islam; if they respond to you, accept it from them and desist from fighting against them. Then invite them to migrate from their lands to the land of Muhairs and inform them that, if they do so, they shall have all the privileges and obligations of the Muhajirs.

If they refuse to migrate, tell them that they will have the status of Bedouin Muslims and will be subjected to the Commands of Allah like other Muslims, but they will not get any share from the spoils of war or Fai' except when they actually fight with the Muslims (against the disbelievers).

If they refuse to accept Islam, demand from them the Jizya. If they agree to pay, accept it from them and hold off your hands. If they refuse to pay the tax, seek Allah's help and fight them.

When you lay siege to a fort and the besieged appeal to you for protection in the name of Allah and His Prophet, do not accord to them the guarantee of Allah and His Prophet, but accord to them your own guarantee and the guarantee of your companions for it is a lesser sin that the security given by you or your companions be disregarded than that the security granted in the name of Allah and His Prophet be violated.

When you besiege a fort and the besieged want you to let them out in accordance with Allah's Command, do not let them come out in accordance with His Command, but do so at your (own) command, for you do not know whether or not you will be able to carry out Allah's behest with regard to them.

These are the marching orders for the holy war of Allah. The victims of this war are given three choices. First they can convert to Islam. Second they can migrate from where they live to another land. Or finally, they can become non-Muslim members of the Islamic republic and pay a tax for the privilege.

Unbelievers turn or be second class citizens

Historically non-Muslim peoples in lands ruled by Muslims were second class citizens. Being non-Muslim meant much more than just paying a tax. Andrew G. Bostom gives us the details in his December 30, 2005 article entitled "'Democrats' For Jihad and Jizya" found at www.americanthinker.com.

The "contract of the 'jizya," or "dhimma" encompassed other obligatory and recommended obligations for the conquered non-Muslim "dhimmi" peoples. Collectively, these "obliga-tions" formed the discriminatory system of dhimmitude imposed upon non-Muslims — Jews, Christians, Zoroastrians, Hindus, and Buddhists — subjugated by jihad. Some of the more salient features of dhimmitude include:

- *the prohibition of arms for the vanquished non-Muslims (dhimmis);*

- *the prohibition of church bells;*

- *restrictions concerning the building and restoration of churches, synagogues, and temples;*

- *inequality between Muslims and non-Muslims with regard to taxes and penal law;*

- *the refusal of dhimmi testimony by Muslim courts;*

- *a requirement that Jews, Christians, and other non-Muslims, including Zoroastrians and Hindus, wear special clothes;*

- *and the overall humiliation and abasement of non-Muslims.*

I could not find any instances of Modern Muslim states imposing the "Jizya" tax, but there are Muslims that have called for the return to these practices. Certainly non-Muslims living in a majority Muslim country are treated as second class citizens in many ways. The population of Pakistan is about 97 percent Muslim. Here are some recent examples of how non-Muslims are treated in Pakistan. These excerpts were found on www.wikislam.com.

On May 30, 2007, Younis Masih, a Christian, was sentenced to death under Section 295C of the Pakistan Penal Code, accused of committing blasphemy against the Prophet Mohammed.

In May 2007, a community of approximately 500 Christians in Charsadda, North-West Frontier Province, were given an ultimatum to convert to Islam by 17 May, or face "dire consequences." Threats were repeated on a wall opposite a church, and similar threats have been made in other towns.

September 6, 2004

Second Pakistani Christian tortured to death by police in four months. Another Christian has died in Pakistan as a result of severe torture at the hands of the police. This is the third murder of a Pakistani Christian this year, and the second carried out by the police.

Nasir Masih, aged 26, was arrested on false charges of theft ... and died three days later after sustaining 20 injuries. According to his father, Mukhtar Masih, Nasir was taken from his home in Baldia, Siekhupura, 45 kilometers from Lahore, by a group of Muslims, and a few hours later his family was informed by the police that he had been arrested and charged with theft. The accusation had been made by one of the group which took Nasir from his home.

"This is a conspiracy based on religious enmity to kill my son," Mukhtar Masih told the All Pakistan Minorities Alliance. "My son cannot have been involved in any theft." A case has been registered against ten people, including six policemen, for allegedly torturing Nasir Masih to death, on the orders of the District Police Officer Shahid Iqbal. No arrests have yet been made. "I will knock on every door to get justice for my son," Mukhtar Masih said.

Nasir's murder follows the deaths ... of Samuel Masih and Javed Anjum. Samuel Masih, charged under the blasphemy law, was beaten by a police officer while he lay in a hospital suffering from tuberculosis. Javed Anjum was tortured to death by Muslims from a madrassah (Islamic school).

Hundreds of Christians protested Nasir Masih's murder by blocking the Siekhupura to Lahore road on August 20. Police responded to the protest with a baton charge and firing in the air, which led to several protestors being injured. Police beat up and arrested Pastor Joel Raja and Pastor Noel Cecil, who were preparing to lead Nasir Masih's funeral, along with 15 others.

The two pastors and five others have been released, but ten further people remain in police custody. Police have also warned the local Christian community, particularly Haroon Fateh, a lawyer representing Nasih Masih's family, not to pursue the case against the police. About a dozen Christian protestors have been charged with suspending traffic and rioting.

May 21, 2003

A nine-year-old Christian girl from Pakistan claims to have been beaten and sexually assaulted by her Muslim employers whenever footage from the war in Iraq was shown on television. The girl from Faisal Town in Lahore claims that when she cried for mercy, they would ask her to call for the Americans to help her.

She said the couple told her they were taking revenge for the American bombing of Iraqi Muslim children on her because she was an "infidel and a Christian," according to what she told CSW partners, the All Pakistan Minorities Alliance (APMA), a human rights NGO based in Pakistan.

She said the couple would beat her with a cricket bat, hang her upside down from the ceiling, pour spoonfuls of hot chilies into her mouth, handcuff her and bash her head repeatedly against the wall. When she cried and appealed for mercy, they would tell her to call the Americans for help.

She attempted to escape from her employers on April 26, but after being recaptured, she was so badly beaten that she was put on a rickshaw to her home by her employers who apparently thought she would die. When her older brother took her to the local hospital, she was immediately admitted to the intensive care unit. A preliminary medical report from that hospital stated that she had suffered a fractured right arm, multiple burns, and bruises and lacerations to her face and body.

She was later treated at Jinnah Hospital, Lahore and is suffering from depression and trauma.

Islam gives its followers a blessing to strike out at the non-Muslim minorities making it part of Allah's will to use force against the unbelievers.

Until death do us part

Once someone becomes a Muslim, force is used to keep him or her in the family. An apostate is someone who has been a follower of the faith and then has decided to leave the religion. This would include a convert to Islam who leaves the faith. It would also apply to children who are raised Muslim and decide to leave the faith when they are adults.

The following passages from the Hadith show clearly that Islam demands the death of anyone who has decided to leave it. Apostates are to be killed. There is no freedom of conscience with this faith. Force and violence are used to lead people to the faith. Force and violence are used to keep them in the Islamic Faith.

It makes me wonder how many people are kept in Islam by the threat of death. At www.faithfreedom.org you can read testimonials of men and women who have left Islam. Many of them believe that if the threat of death were removed from Islam, Muslims would leave the faith in large numbers.

Bukhari Hadith Volume 4, Book 52, Number 260
Narrated by Ikrima

Ali burnt some people and this news reached Ibn 'Abbas, who said, "Had I been in his place I would not have burnt them, as the Prophet said, 'Don't punish (anybody) with Allah's Punishment.' No doubt, I would have killed them, for the Prophet said, 'If somebody (a Muslim) discards his religion, kill him.' "

Bukhari Hadith Volume 9, Book 83, Number 37
Narrated by Abu Qilaba

By Allah, Allah's Apostle never killed anyone except in one of the following three situations: (1) A person who killed somebody unjustly, was killed (in Qisas,) (2) a married person who committed illegal sexual intercourse and (3) a man who fought against Allah and His Apostle and deserted Islam and became an apostate.

Bukhari Hadith Volume 9, Book 89, Number 271
Narrated by Abu Musa

A man embraced Islam and then reverted back to Judaism. Mu'adh bin Jabal came and saw the man with Abu Musa. Mu'adh asked, "What is wrong with this (man)?" Abu Musa replied, "He embraced Islam and then reverted back to Judaism." Mu'adh said, "I will not sit down unless you kill him (as it is) the verdict of Allah and His Apostle."

Muhammad commanded that Apostates be killed and he personally murdered them. Here is yet another example of Islam using force against those, who because of freedom of conscience, no longer wish to submit to Allah. Today, Muslims continue this use of force or the threat of force just as their prophet would have wanted.

According to the 2002 State Department's International Religious Freedom Report, renouncing Islam is by law, punishable by death in Saudi Arabia, Qatar, Yemen, Iran, Sudan and Mauritania.

Mark A. Gabriel on page 18 of his book, *Islam and Terrorism,* tells us his story of leaving Islam. Here is what happened when he told his father his decision.

First, my father fainted right there on the street. Some of my brothers rushed out to him, and my mother started crying in fear. I stayed with them as they bathed my father's face with water. When he came to, he was so upset he could hardly speak, but he pointed at me. In a voice hoarse with rage he cried out, "Your Brother is a convert, I must kill him today!"

Wherever he went, my father carried a gun under his arm on a leather strap. (Most wealthy people in Egypt carry guns.) He pulled out his gun and pointed it at me. I started running down the street, and as I dove around a corner, I heard the bullets whining past me. I kept running for my life.

This next story, found at www.faithfreedom.org, is a January 8, 2005 testimonial by Sahid entitled "I am a Saudi ex-Muslim." Sahid confirms the State Department report by indicating that in Saudi Arabia he would have been killed for leaving Islam. He cannot tell his family who still live in Saudi Arabia about his decision because they would not react well to his apostasy.

The 9/11 Verses

Dear Ali Sina,

Sorry for bad English but I needed to write to you. I am not very good at it. I am a Muslim. I read your articles and changed my mind about Islam. I was among those who tried to advocate Islam. I thought Osama bin Laden was not a Muslim and I was. Now I see I was not a Muslim and Osama Bin Laden was.

Fortunately I am living in Sweden and I can become an apostate. It is a free country. I was born in Saudi Arabia and if I left Islam in that country I would be killed.

I must change my whole life because I left Islam. It will be hard, but I will try to do it because I don't want to be a Muslim. I no longer visit mosque. I no longer pray. I stopped doing these things. I shaved my face.

I don't promise to become a Western man in a day, but I already began changing. My family is living in Saudi Arabia. I will not tell them about my decision because they are very intolerant. I hope all Muslims will leave Islam. And it will happen. Islam is inhumane. You can't be a human and a Muslim at the same time. Most Muslims will choose to be humans. It is for sure.

I was a Muslim, but I didn't want to kill non-Muslims. I didn't think about such verses in the Quran. I thought it was to be practiced only in the 7th century.

I am a father. I have a one-year-old daughter. Her mother died when she was having her. My daughter will not be a Muslim woman. She will be a western woman. She will receive education and have a career. I will do everything I can to do it.

What do you think Sahid means when he says that he thought Osama Bin Laden was not a Muslim? Before Sahid really opened his eyes to the force and violence that is a part of Islam, he thought of Osama as an extremist. Now he sees Bin Laden as a true Muslim. Osama is practicing what the Muslim faith teaches in the Koran and Hadith.

Sahid says, "now I see I was not a Muslim." In other words even though he practiced some of the Islamic faith he truly was not a Muslim because he did not want to be involved with the force and violence that Muhammad commanded.

If you think that Muslim thoughts of force against apostates are limited to Islamic countries, then look at this April 22, 2007 story, found on www.littlegreenfootballs.com, entitled "Pittsburgh Islamic Leader: Ayaan Hirsi Ali Should Be Killed." This is happening right here in the United States. Here are some excerpts.

When ex-Muslim Ayaan Hirsi Ali appeared at the University of Pittsburgh at Johnstown, Muslim groups tried to have her speech shut down. And they made it clear that if they had the power, and U.S. law were written according to shari'a, Hirsi Ali would not simply be prohibited from speaking. According to the president of the Johnstown Islamic Center, Imam Fouad ElBayly, she'd be dead.

Islamic leaders attempted to have the lecture censored. University officials declined to shut down the speech by Ayaan Hirsi Ali. The president of the Johnstown Islamic Center, Imam Fouad ElBayly, strongly objected to the lecture. The Imam stated that Ayaan had defamed the faith. Since Ayaan was once a Muslim then she must forever abide by the rules of the faith. The sentence for deliberately defaming Islam is death.

Imam ElBayly called for the extradition of Ayaan to a Muslim country to be tried in an Islamic court of law for her "crime." The Imam stated that Islam is very merciful since, if Ayaan was found to be mentally unstable, she would not be executed.

Islamic leaders here in this country would, if they could, impose the death penalty on ex-Muslims as the prophet commanded. American Islamic leaders tried to take away the American right to free speech by attempting to have the lecture canceled. Why are Muslims so afraid of a free and open exchange of ideas? Why do they need to use threats and force to keep Islam going? I thank God that courageous people have refused to be intimidated from discussing these issues. Is Islam so weak that it cannot withstand the light of debate?

The president of the Islamic center agrees with my inter-pretation that Muhammad commands death for apostates. If these Muslims had the power they would imposes Islamic Sharia law in this country. Sharia law takes the religious rules of Islam and writes them into the law of the land. This would accomplish a complete merging of church and state into one nation under Allah.

True faith cannot be forced

I was amazed by the holy writings of Islam's call for the use of forced conversions. From the stories presented in this chapter, it is clear that the modern day application of these verses of force is horrifying. True faith comes from a voluntary free choice and cannot be forced.

It seems to me that a relationship of faith with God is one of the most close and intimate types of connections that one can have. It is a connection that comes from the heart of the believer not from someone else's heart.

I cannot force someone to love, or respect me. Love, and respect comes as a voluntary choice. Force is for children. The immature need to be shown discipline. As parents are raising their children, they force them to do things they do not want to do.

Most children do not want to clean their rooms or go to bed at a certain time. Loving parents provide training and structure to prepare children to be able to make good choices as adults. Choice is for adults. Choice to commit yourself to a faith is personal and profound. Conversions under threats are not real. Over one-third of the planet claims faith in Christ. All voluntarily without threats or force.

The Islamic zealots that roam the earth trying to force Muslim views onto the rest of us are like unthinking, emotionally immature children. Children go along with the faith environment that is in their home. If a child's parents go to church, the child goes with them. Very young children learn the faith of their parents without much thought or questioning. There comes a point in time when older children begin to question what they have been taught. At some point they decide whether or not to continue in the faith tradition that they have been raised in.

Part of becoming an adult is exercising your own choices in matters of faith. When this happens your faith decisions are coming from true and sincere beliefs – not just following others.

Islam maintains itself by threats and force. For many Muslims this does not allow for a freely chosen faith. Abdullah Qasim, a former Muslim, began to question his faith. He became an adult in his thinking about Islam by putting the claims of his teachers to the test. Here are some excerpts from comments by him in an August 31, 2007 article entitled, "My Reasons Why I Quit Islam Forever," posted online at www.islam-watch.org.

I was born in a devout Muslim family belonging to Sunni sect of Islam. I come from an Islamic country, but currently I live in a western country. During every Ramadan I used to faithfully fast. During my University study, one of my subjects was Islamic Studies. My professor of the subject glorified Islam and taught all the good deeds of the prophet of Islam.

I was taught that Quran is the perfect and the best book sent by God. Islam should be dominant and supersede all the religions of the world. However I realized that he never mentioned why the prophet was so violent and killed so many people.

The Islamic teachings that I received were accepted totally by me in the beginning. I defended Islam at all costs. I hated anyone who criticized the prophet or Islam. However, when I read 23 Years of Prophet by Ali Dashti, and when I went through various websites like www.Answering-islam.org, www.faithfreedom.org, and the Prophetofdoom.net, and had discussions with non-Muslims, I began to lift my head out of the sand. I started analyzing the Quran and the Islamic teachings, and I realized that the mullahs and the Islamic scholars were hoodwinking the Muslims.

From my childhood I hated violence in any form. To my utter dismay I found out that the Quran is full of violence.

Islam teaches to kill its apostates. Quran 4:89 emphatically states that all apostates in Islam should be killed. Many references in hadith show that ex-Muslims were killed and are to be killed.

Abdullah Qasim
www.islam-watch.org

Qasim goes on to make many other excellent points which makes his article worth the time to read. The teaching received by him during his upbringing was clear to him. Islam is about force and violence. The Internet contains many other writings by ex-Muslims that testify to the same. As Qasim writes, Islam uses force to keep you in the faith once you convert. If you decide to leave Islam the Koran says you should be killed.

Forced to faith

United States' law recognizes that decisions and agreements made under force (duress) are not valid. This is because the agreement has not been freely made. If someone holds a gun to your head and has you sign a contract to sell them your house, the sale would not be legally valid. This is because the house sale agreement was not entered into freely or without undue pressure.

When it comes to conversion, Islam does not recognize duress as making the conversion invalid. Conversions by force have been historically, and are still today, part of the faith. Robert Spencer sheds light on this in his August 30, 2006 piece entitled "Journalists' Forced Conversion Not Contrary to Islam" found at www.HumanEvents.com.

> *Muhammad instructed his followers to call people to Islam before waging war against them—the warfare would follow from their refusal to accept Islam or to enter the Islamic social order as inferiors, required to pay a special tax (Sahih Muslim 4294). There is therefore a threat in this "invitation" to accept Islam.*
>
> *Would one who converted to Islam under the threat of war be considered to have converted under duress? No; from the standpoint of traditional schools of Islamic jurisprudence, such a conversion would have resulted from "no compulsion."*

In August 2006, Fox news reporter Steve Centanni and his cameraman Olaf Wiig were kidnapped in Gaza by Muslims. They were forced to convert to Islam at gunpoint and a video of their "conversion" was distributed. This is just one story among hundreds. Muslims are still today using force to obtain "conversions" to their faith.

Those who use force and violence to advance the Islamic faith are doing so to follow the will of Allah and his messenger. The words and deeds of the founder of their faith approve what they do. Force is used to gain conversions. Force is used to destroy or enslave those who refuse to convert. Force is used to keep Muslims from leaving the faith.

The 9/11 Verses

It cannot be denied that commands to force Islamic beliefs on non-Muslims is a major element of the Islamic faith that leads to acts of terrorism like 9/11. As Muhammad might say if he were here today "unbelievers turn or burn!"

For Me To Die Is Paradise!

> *Teacher which is the greatest commandment in the law?*
> *Jesus replied: "Love the Lord your God with all your*
> *heart and with all your soul and with all your mind.*
> *This is the first and greatest commandment. And the second*
> *is like it: Love your neighbor as yourself. All the Law and*
> *the Prophets hang on these two commandments."*
> Matthew 22:36-40

> *A man came to Allah's Apostle and said,*
> *"Instruct me as to such a deed as equals Jihad in reward."*
> *He replied, "I do not find such a deed."*
> Muhammad

This chapter is about the fourth and final major element of Islam that causes its followers to commit violent acts. Muhammad must have understood human nature very well. Built into Islam is a great incentive to kill, hurt and otherwise harm non-Muslims. A great reward is absolutely, positively guaranteed for Muslims who die for Allah. Dying for Allah while fighting and killing others is a sure ticket to paradise. Family members who are left behind also receive rewards in the next life as a result of the Muslim martyr's actions.

In this chapter, I will uncover the verses that promise rewards for dying for Allah. Apologists for Islam will say that these verses are being misapplied or interpreted wrongly. However, I think you will see there are clear and straightforward. When you combine them with Muhammad's own words and actions, their application and meaning cannot be denied.

Perhaps the best test of the interpretation of these passages is to examine the thoughts of modern day Muslims who are planning to die for Allah. As you read their stories you will find their interpretations of the verses you read here. As you will see what Islamic Jihadists think, say, and do is not made up out of thin air. It is a direct result of their knowledge of the Holy Scriptures of Islam.

Blessed are the war-makers

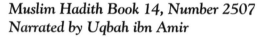

Muslim Hadith Book 14, Number 2507
Narrated by Uqbah ibn Amir

I heard the Apostle of Allah (peace be upon him) say: Allah, Most High, will cause three persons to enter Paradise for one arrow: the maker when he has a good motive in making it, the one who shoots it, and the one who hands it; so shoot and ride, but your shooting is dearer to me than your riding.

Muslim Hadith Book 14, Number 2520
Narrated by Abdullah ibn Amr ibn al-'As

The Prophet (peace be upon him) said: The warrior gets his reward, and the one who equips him gets his own reward and that of the warrior.

I can picture the terrorist making suicide vests happily knowing that his work will gain him the reward of heaven. In fact he is extra happy because he not only gets his own reward but also that of the warrior who wears the vest and blows up infidels. He gets both rewards and as a bonus is still alive to continue to make more weapons and rack up additional reward points from future warriors dying in the cause of Allah.

The young boy who wears the vest, blows himself up, and kills infidels is motivated by the Apostle of Allah's word that he will enter paradise in reward for his efforts.

Here is a look into the mind of a dedicated Muslim Jihad fighter. Aaron Klein, from www.Worldnetdaily.com in a November 24, 2006 article entitled, "'Hi, my name is Ahmed and I want to be a suicide bomber.'" Here are some excerpts from the interview with the 23-year-old Palestinian man.

WND: Why do you want to become a suicide bomber?

BOMBER: I originally decided to become a martyr after I saw what the Israeli army did in the refugee camp of Jenin in the big military campaign of April, 2002. But this idea became stronger when I understood what status I will have in heaven if I sacrifice myself for Allah. Every time somebody else dies as a martyr in a suicide bomb attack, I pray for him but I feel jealous. I want to be where he is now and I pray that Allah will one day offer me this occasion and this honor.

WND: Is your main motivation for becoming a bomber is to serve Allah?

BOMBER: Yes, of course. Allah gave Muslims the possibility to gain their prize and payment in different ways. There are those (Muslims) who pray and fast only and respect Allah's commandments, and there are those who wish a higher prize. And the highest prize is given to those who sacrifice themselves, their lives, their bodies and everything in this world…

The goal is satisfying Allah and his instructions. No money interests, nothing. No brainwash, no pressure; it is my decision. All the other lies are pathetic Israeli propaganda. I pray that Allah gives me the honor to be dead in an operation. This is the supreme and the noblest way to ascend to Allah.

These martyrs have special status in the next world and have bigger chances to watch Allah's face and enjoy the magnificent pleasures he offers us.

WND: Let's say your concept of heaven is accurate. You are indeed rewarded with 72 dark-eyed virgins for living the kind of life you describe. Do you really think you will go to heaven for killing innocent civilians during a suicide operation?

BOMBER: You are treating, in a ridiculous way, this issue, but this is in the Quran. Go and, Allah forbid, ask Allah about this point. We are promised in the Quran to have the dark-eyed virgins and that's it. The Quran is full of verses glorifying the shahid, the martyr.

WND: Show me exactly where in the Quran it states you will get 72 dark-eyed virgins for blowing yourself up amongst civilians.

BOMBER: You and I, we do not discuss Allah and the Quran. I will tell you more the moment that I will explode myself, then there will be one dark-eyed virgin who will carry up my soul to the sky.

Muhammad, quoted at the start of this chapter, says that the deed of Jihad gets the highest reward. The terrorist bomber understands this teaching and says that the highest prize is given to those who sacrifice their lives for Allah. His motivation originally was anger at the Israeli army. But now his sole reason to kill and die is the "status I will have in heaven." The bomber reads the Koran and concludes correctly that it is full of verses glorifying the martyr.

When Muhammad started the Islamic faith, the number of his believers was small and the world around him was hostile. With

Allah's blessing Muhammad fought and killed to spread his faith. Islam glorifies war for Allah. The scriptures of Islam say in effect "blessed are the war-makers."

In contrast to the Koran's many verses that "glorify the martyr," we have in the New Testament many passages that commend those who live at peace with others. These verses were written at a time when Christianity was just starting. The number of believers was small and they faced a world that was sometimes hostile to them. Here are some examples of New Testament verses that promote peace with others.

✠

If it is possible, as far as it depends on you, live at peace with everyone. **Romans 12:18**

Make every effort to live in peace with all men and to be holy; without holiness no one will see the Lord. **Hebrews 12:14**

Blessed are the peacemakers, for they will be called sons of God. **Matthew 5:9**

For our struggle is not against flesh and blood, but against the rulers, against the authorities, against the powers of this dark world and against the spiritual forces of evil in the heavenly realms. **Ephesians 6:12**

This last verse lets the Christian know that the fight is not "against flesh and blood" but is a spiritual fight. A martyr in the Christian faith is one who is persecuted and killed for belief in Christ. This has happened to Christians since the beginning of the faith up to today. A Christian martyr does not fight and kill others for his faith.

Do I really get 72 virgins?

As the future suicide bomber said, the Koran does promise beautiful virgins for men in paradise. There are many references that describe what these women are like. Here are a few samples.

But, for the Allah-fearing is a blissful abode, enclosed gardens and vineyards; and damsels with swelling breasts, peers in age...   **The Koran, Chapter 78:31**

And theirs shall be the Houris, with large dark eyes, like pearls hidden in their shells...   **The Koran, Chapter 56:22**

But the pious shall be in a secure place, amid gardens and fountains, clothed in silk and richest robes, facing one another. Thus it shall be: and We will wed them to the virgins with large dark eyes.   **The Koran, Chapter 44:51-54**

The Koran makes no reference to the number of virgins for each man being 72. This comes from a Hadith reference by Al-Tirmidhi. Some Muslims believe this quote, while others do not believe it is reliable. Clearly, most terrorists on suicide missions do believe the quote is from Muhammad.

Al-Tirmidhi Hadith 2687

Mohammad said: The least reward for the people of paradise is 80,000 servants and 72 wives.

Allah will also give men the sexual stamina to enjoy sex with many virgins.

Al-Tirmidhi Hadith 5636
Narrated by Anas ibn Malik

The Prophet (peace be upon him) said, "In Paradise, the believer will be given such and such power to conduct sexual intercourse." He was asked whether he would be capable of that and replied that he would be given the capacity of a hundred men.

While the exact number of virgins given each Muslim man who enters paradise may be in question, the scriptures of Islam are clear that sexual pleasures await men in Allah's Paradise.

One ticket to paradise please

You will not find within the pages of the Bible (both Old and New Testament) any teaching that you will get a guaranteed ticket to heaven for fighting in a holy war for God. The Bible teaches that salvation is found through what Christ did for us on the cross. Salvation which includes entrance into heaven is by grace and is a gift to us from God. Grace is something God gives us for free that has nothing to do with us earning it. We cannot accomplish some great deed for God to merit grace. No one can brag or boast about being in heaven because all are there due to God's gift.

✝

For it is by grace you have been saved, through faith and this not from yourselves, it is the gift of God, not by works, so that no one can boast.   **Ephesians 2:8-9**

The Koran and Hadith teach that you will gain heaven if you die for Allah in Jihad. In the Bible the word martyr appears twice.

121

The 9/11 Verses

The holy writings of Islam contain the word martyr many times. A martyr in the Bible is not killed while fighting and trying to kill others. In Islam a martyr is killed while fighting in The Holy War against non-Muslims. These next quotes from Muhammad and the Koran show the assurance of heaven given to the martyr.

Muslim Hadith Book 14, Number 2515
Narrated by Hasana' daughter of Mu'awiyah

She reported on the authority of her paternal uncle: I asked the Prophet (peace be upon him): Who are in Paradise? He replied: Prophets are in Paradise, martyrs are in Paradise, infants are in Paradise and children buried alive are in Paradise.

Muslim Hadith Book 14, Number 2535
Narrated by Mu'adh ibn Jabal

The Apostle of Allah (peace be upon him) said: If anyone fights in Allah's path as long as the time between two milkings of a she-camel, Paradise will be assured for him. If anyone sincerely asks Allah for being killed and then dies or is killed, there will be a reward of a martyr for him.

Ibn al-Musaffa added from here: If anyone is wounded in Allah's path, or suffers a misfortune, it will come on the Day of Resurrection as copious as possible, its color saffron, and its odor musk; and if anyone suffers from ulcers while in Allah's path, he will have on him the stamp of the martyrs.

Verily, of the faithful hath Allah bought their persons and their substance, on condition of Paradise for them in return:

on the path of Allah shall they fight, and slay, and be slain...Rejoice, therefore in the contract that ye have contracted: for this shall be a great bliss.

The Koran, Chapter 9:112

Bukhari Hadith Volume 4, Book 52, Number 46
Narrated by Abu Huraira

I heard Allah's Apostle saying, "The example of a Mujahid in Allah's Cause — and Allah knows better who really strives in His Cause — is like a person who fasts and prays continuously. Allah guarantees that He will admit the Mujahid in His Cause into Paradise if he is killed, otherwise He will return him to his home safely with rewards and war booty."

Bukhari Hadith Volume 4, Book 52, Number 73
Narrated by 'Abdullah bin Abi Aufa

Allah's Apostle said, "Know that Paradise is under the shades of swords."

Some modern Muslims try to downplay the idea of physically fighting and dying for Allah. They talk about Jihad as a "spiritual struggle." They are dishonest if they ignore and fail to explain these verses. Clearly Muhammad is commanding physical fighting and killing.

In an April 5, 2004 article entitled "Britain's Suicide Bombers: The Real Story" found at www.bbc.co.uk, a modern Muslim leader gives us his interpretation of the writings of Islam and "self sacrifice operations."

This leader's name is Omar Bakri, and he is calling on Muslims in Britain to fight against their non-Muslim fellow citizens. Bakri has spoke in favor of the Madrid Bombers. His justification is that

Spain was being paid back, "eye for and eye, tooth for tooth, life for life," for its participation in the Iraq war. He has called on British Muslims to "kill and be killed" for the sake of Islam. He tells young British Muslims that "suicide bombers would be guaranteed a place in paradise."

Bakri makes direct appeals to Muslims to commit terrorist acts. He says that Islam gives approval to their actions. Here are a few excerpts from the article.

> *He instructs his followers to take direct action.*
>
> > *"Prepare as much as you can from strength and from force to terrorize — because terrorism it is part of Islam."*
>
> *At an earlier meeting the BBC recorded Omar Bakri encouraging members of his British audience to become suicide bombers.*
>
> > *"Martyrdom is what you want. Do the effort. Clear your intention. Go forward, never look backwards. Make sure you have nothing left behind you to think about or cry for and fight in the name of Allah."*
>
> *He refers to suicide missions as self-sacrifice operations.*
>
> > *"So what is self-sacrifice operation? It's got to be the following scenario. Somebody he flies an aeroplane and he decides to land the aeroplane over 10 Downing Street, for example, or over the White House. This is a form of self-sacrifice operation."*

Bakri clearly believes in the guarantee of paradise for those who die while killing for Allah. Of course he does not do what he is asking others to do. It seems the leaders always live on while encouraging others to die.

How sweet it is to be martyred

Islam gives the largest reward for Jihad. I would think that the first, second, and third place ribbons would be awarded for acts of kindness and love. How about rewards for feeding the hungry, taking care of an elderly parent, bringing medical care to the poorest of the world, or helping to fight AIDS. What about a first place award for starting and growing a successful company that provides good jobs and excellent products? No! Instead Islam gives the first place award for acts of violence and killing.

Bukhari Hadith Volume 4, Book 52, Number 44
Narrated by Abu Huraira

A man came to Allah's Apostle and said, "Instruct me as to such a deed as equals Jihad in reward." He replied, "I do not find such a deed."

Bukhari Hadith Volume 4, Book 52, Number 50
Narrated by Anas bin Malik

The Prophet said, "A single endeavor (of fighting) in Allah's Cause in the forenoon or in the afternoon is better than the world and whatever is in it."

Bukhari Hadith Volume 4, Book 52, Number 63
Narrated by Al-Bara

A man whose face was covered with an iron mask (i.e. clad in armor) came to the Prophet and said, "O Allah's Apostle! Shall I fight or embrace Islam first?" The Prophet said, "Embrace Islam first and then fight." So he embraced Islam, and was martyred. Allah's Apostle said, A little work, but a great reward. "(He did very little (after embracing Islam), but he will be rewarded in abundance)."

What is the greatest deed?

The following Hadith stories honor being a martyr as the highest good and the most superior action you can take with your life. In the quote at the beginning of this chapter Jesus said that the greatest thing you can do is to love God with all your heart, soul and mind and love your neighbor like you do yourself. Jesus says that all the law and the prophets hang on loving God and your neighbor. This means that everything God wants us to do is designed to show us how to love. All the commands in the Bible are intended to give us detailed instructions on how to love God and others. According to Christ love is the greatest deed.

Bukhari Hadith Volume 4, Book 52, Number 53
Narrated by Anas bin Malik

The Prophet said, "Nobody who dies and finds good from Allah (in the Hereafter) would wish to come back to this world even if he were given the whole world and whatever is in it, except the martyr who, on seeing the superiority of martyrdom, would like to come back to the world and get killed again (in Allah's Cause)."

Bukhari Hadith Volume 4, Book 52, Number 64
Narrated by Anas bin Malik

Um Ar-Rubai'bint Al-Bara', the mother of Hartha bin Suraqa came to the Prophet and said, "O Allah's Prophet! Will you tell me about Hartha?" Hartha has been killed (i.e. martyred) on the day of Badr with an arrow thrown by an unidentified person. She added, "If he is in Paradise, I will be patient; otherwise, I will weep bitterly for him." He said, "O mother of Hartha! There are Gardens in Paradise and your son got the Firdausal-ala (i.e. the best place in Paradise)."

Bukhari Hadith Volume 4, Book 52, Number 72
Narrated by Anas bin Malik

The Prophet said, "Nobody who enters Paradise likes to go back to the world even if he got everything on the earth, except a Mujahid who wishes to return to the world so that he may be martyred ten times because of the dignity he receives (from Allah)."

Narrated by Al-Mughira bin Shu'ba

Our Prophet told us about the message of our Lord that "Whoever amongst us is killed will go to Paradise." Umar asked the Prophet, "Is it not true that our men who are killed will go to Paradise and theirs (i.e. those of the Pagan's) will go to the (Hell) fire?" The Prophet said, "Yes."

Terrorist bomber knows — martyrdom is superior

Here is a July 14, 2004 story, found at www.Jihadwatch.org, entitled "The BBC Interviews a Suicide Bomber." This is a BBC interview with would be terrorist bomber Hussam Abdo. Hussam clearly knows the Islamic teaching of the superiority of martyrdom.

JR: When you put on that belt, did you really know — as a 15-year-old — that you were going to go and murder people, that you were going to go and cause great suffering to mothers and fathers, that you were going to be a mass murderer? Did you really know that?

Hussam: Yes. Just like they came and caused our parents sadness and suffering, they too should feel this. Just like we feel this — they should also feel it.

JR: Some teenagers want to be footballers, others want to be singers. You wanted to be a suicide bomber. Why?

Hussam: It's not suicide – it's martyrdom. I would become a martyr and go to my God. It's better than being a singer or a footballer. It's better than everything.

Muslim mother rejoices over son who killed

This next article is taken from a January 8, 2003 commentary at www.womensenews.org entitled, "Mothers of Suicide Bombers May Only Defer Grief," by Peggy F. Drexler, Ph.D. The piece shows the joy of a Muslim mother when her son has become a martyr. She is convinced that to be a martyr is superior. Her pride in her son's "accomplishment" is plain to see. As a parent I would be proud of my child's positive accomplishment in academics, or career or relationships. But this mother, having been taught by Islam, is happy with Her son's destructive act.

"I was very happy when I heard," said the wife of Bashir al-Masawabi, the mother of suicide bomber Ismail al-Masawabi, in an interview with Joseph Lelyveld, former managing editor of The New York Times for a piece in the newspaper's Sunday magazine.

Speaking from the relatively roomy flat she had just moved into, courtesy of Hamas, the radical Palestinian group that recruited Ismail, she added, "To be a martyr, that's something very few people can do. I prayed to thank God."

Ismail's mother appeared remarkably absent of grief. "In the Koran it's said that a martyr does not die," she stated. "I know my son is close to me."

Suicide bombers smile before blowing up

Pierre Rehov is a documentary filmmaker who has gone undercover in Muslim areas to gather information for his films. He has conducted extensive interviews of suicide bombers and their families and victims who survived. According to Pierre, victims have described again and again that the suicide bombers are "all smiling one second before they blow themselves up."

I believe this is because they are anticipating the reward promised by Islam. They are eager for the dark eyed virgins to carry them to the best place in paradise. The pleasures of Allah blessed sex with many beautiful virgins will be theirs to claim.

Here are some enlightening excerpts from the interview with Pierre Rehov entitled "Suicide Killers The Psychology Behind Suicide Bombings" found on www.usadojo.com.

Q - What was it like to interview would-be suicide bombers, their families and survivors of suicide bombings?

A - It was a fascinating and a terrifying experience. You are dealing with seemingly normal people with very nice manners who have their own logic, which to a certain extent can make sense since they are so convinced that what they say is true. It is like dealing with pure craziness, like interviewing people in an asylum, since what they say, is for them, the absolute truth.

I hear a mother saying "Thank God, my son is dead." Her son had became a shaheed, a martyr, which for her was a greater source of pride than if he had became an engineer, a doctor or a winner of the Nobel Prize.

This system of values works completely backwards since their interpretation of Islam worships death much more than life. You are facing people whose only dream, only achievement goal is to fulfill what they believe to be their destiny, namely to be a Shaheed or the family of a Shaheed.

They don't see the innocent being killed, they only see the impure that they have to destroy.

Q - Are suicide bombers principally motivated by religious conviction?

A - Yes, it is their only conviction. They don't act to gain a territory or to find freedom or even dignity. They only follow Allah, the supreme judge, and what He tells them to do.

Q - Do all Muslims interpret jihad and martyrdom in the same way?

A - All Muslim believers believe that, ultimately, Islam will prevail on earth. They believe this is the only true religion and there is no room, in their mind, for interpretation. The main difference between moderate Muslims and extremists is that moderate Muslims don't think they will see the absolute victory of Islam during their lifetime, therefore they respect other beliefs. The extremists believe that the fulfillment of the Prophecy of Islam and ruling the entire world as described in the Koran, is for today. Each victory of Bin Laden convinces 20 million moderate Muslims to become extremists.

Pierre Rehov Interview
<u>www.usadojo.com</u>

Muhammad takes on the power to forgive sins

Bukhari Hadith Volume 4, Book 52, Number 175
Narrated by Khalid bin Madan

That 'Umair bin Al-Aswad Al-Anasi told him that he went to 'Ubada bin As-Samit while he was staying in his house at the sea-shore of Hims with (his wife) Um Haram. 'Umair said. Um Haram informed us that she heard the Prophet saying, "Paradise is granted to the first batch of my followers who will undertake a naval expedition." Um Haram added, "I said, 'O Allah's Apostle! Will I be amongst them?' He replied, 'You are amongst them.' The Prophet then said, 'The first army amongst my followers who will invade Caesar's City will be forgiven their sins.' I asked, 'Will I be one of them, O Allah's Apostle?' He replied in the negative."

In this story the prophet promises the forgiveness of sins for the first army of his followers to invade Caesar's City. That Muhammad takes on himself the power to forgive sins is amazing. During his ministry on earth Jesus got in a lot of trouble for the same thing. On several occasions he told people their sins were forgiven. This caused a problem with the religious leaders who knew that forgiving sins was something that only God can do. Look at this story from gospel of Luke.

✠

One day as he was teaching, Pharisees and teachers of the law, who had come from every village of Galilee and from Judea and Jerusalem, were sitting there. And the power of the Lord was present for him to heal the sick. Some men came carrying a paralytic on a mat and tried to take him into the house to lay him before Jesus. When they could not find a way to do this because of the crowd, they went up on the roof and lowered him on his mat through the tiles into the middle of the crowd, right in front of Jesus.

When Jesus saw their faith, he said, "Friend, your sins are forgiven."

The Pharisees and the teachers of the law began thinking to themselves, "Who is this fellow who speaks blasphemy? Who can forgive sins but God alone?" **Luke 5:17-21**

Muhammad seems to be taking on a power that God alone has. Forgiveness of sins is a powerful inducement to get men to fight and die for you in war.

Martyrdom has a family plan

When a Muslim dies fighting for Allah in Jihad (holy war), he is absolutely guaranteed a place in paradise. Also he gains power as an intercessor to be able to help out up to seventy members of his family. An intercessor is someone who is able to make a petition or request to God on behalf of someone else. The following Hadith passage says that the intercession of a martyr "will be accepted." So the Jihadist can petition Allah to admit his family members into paradise and his petition will be granted.

Muslim Hadith Book 14, Number 2516
Narrated by AbudDarda'

The Prophet (peace be upon him) said: The intercession of a martyr will be accepted for seventy members of his family.

In a November 26, 2006 article in the online edition of the *Jerusalem Post* entitled "Letting Suicide Bombers speak for Themselves," Tom Tugend details a Muslim's view on the family plan of martyrdom. It is obvious that this would be martyr was taught the Hadith that I disclosed above.

Sixteen-year old Hassan is deeply frustrated because he was caught by the Israeli police before he could blow himself up among a crowd of Israeli civilians.

"If I had been killed, my mother would call it a blessing," he says. "My family and 70 relatives would have gone to paradise, and that would be a great honor for me."

In this next story, the prophet hands out rewards to the surviving mother of a "martyr." She gets twice the reward of a martyr. The reason for that is her son was killed in battle by "the people of the book." Islam considers Jews and Christians to be "people of the book." The book is the Bible.

The Christian faith teaches that God is going to judge people based on their own actions not the actions of others. The idea that martyrdom benefits the family members of the jihadist provides additional incentives for mothers and fathers to offer up their sons as a sacrifice for Muhammad's goals of spreading Islam.

Muslim Hadith Book 14, Number 2482
Narrated by Thabit ibn Qays

A woman called Umm Khallad came to the Prophet (peace be upon him) while she was veiled. She was searching for her son who had been killed (in the battle). Some of the Companions of the Prophet (peace be upon him) said to her: You have come here asking for your son while veiling your face? She said: If I am afflicted with the loss of my son, I shall not suffer the loss of my modesty. The Apostle of Allah (peace be upon him) said: You will get the reward of two martyrs for your son. She asked: Why is that so, Apostle of Allah? He replied: Because the people of the Book have killed him.

Jihad or bust

In case all of the positive incentives and inducements to get followers to kill and die for Allah are not enough, the Prophet has the answer. If you do not participate in the warlike expedition of jihad, either directly or in support, then Allah will hit you with a sudden calamity. The messenger of Allah employs both the carrot and the stick.

Muslim Hadith Book 14, Number 2497
Narrated by AbuUmamah

The Prophet (peace be upon him) said: He who does not join the warlike expedition (jihad), or equip, or looks well after a warrior's family when he is away, will be smitten by Allah with a sudden calamity. Yazid ibn Abdu Rabbihi said in his tradition: "before the Day of Resurrection."

Do as I say not as I do

Muhammad sets up a series of inducements to enjoin his followers to fight, kill and die for Allah. As usual this does not seem to apply to the leaders of Islam. Muhammad died of natural causes. He did not die "fighting for Allah." In battles Muhammad would position himself in the back away from the dangerous front lines. He said he did so to "encourage the weak and afraid in the battle." Another of his excuses for staying where it was safe was that there were men who "disliked to be left behind him."

This next story illustrates how Muhammad survived a battle by promising his fighters Paradise that day if they would preserve his life. You can see how Muhammad stays in the back of the fighting while one by one his men go to "Paradise."

Muslim Hadith Book 019, Number 4413

It has been reported on the authority of Anas b. Malik that (when the enemy got the upper hand) on the day of the Battle of Uhud, the Messenger of Allah (may peace be upon him) was left with only seven men from the ansar and two men from the Quraish. When the enemy advanced towards him and overwhelmed him, he said: Whoso turns them away, from us will attain Paradise or will be my Companion in Paradise.

> *A man from the Ansar came forward and fought (the enemy) until he was killed. The enemy advanced and overwhelmed him again and he repeated the words: Whoso turns them away, from us will attain Paradise or will be my Companion in Paradise.*
>
> *A man from the Ansar came forward and fought until he was killed. This state continued until the seven Ansar were killed (one after the other). Now, the Messenger of Allah (may peace be upon him) said to his two Companions: We have not done justice to our Companions.*

Modern Islamic leaders follow the example of the founder of their faith. They do not die for Allah in the way that they ask others to do. Bin Laden hides somewhere in a cave. Ayman al-Zawahri, Bin Laden's second in command, issues videos from wherever he is hiding. These Islamic leaders urge their followers to jihad and martyrdom. Since being a martyr is the greatest deed, why not come out from your caves and die for Allah?

Instead these "leaders" of Islam send others to do Allah's work. As I was writing this chapter, Al-Qaeda used a Downs Syndrome woman to accomplish a "martyr operation" in Iraq. What level of depravity is needed to be able to strap explosives to an innocent mentally disabled human being and kill them by remote control. Hundreds of people were killed or wounded.

For Muslims to kill and die is paradise

No one can deny that the idea of rewards of heaven for killing and dying for Allah is major element of Islam. There can be no other interpretation. There may be different ideas on who it is okay to kill and who it is not okay to kill. Muslims can and do differ on the definition of "terrorist" and "innocent." But just the fact that the Holy Writings of Islam contain these ideas provides a strong motivation in Islam for death and destruction.

The 9/11 Verses

I have not found in any other major faith anything like the Islamic concept of rewards for a follower and his family for killing and dying for God. Christianity, Hinduism, Buddhism, and modern Judaism do not put forth this concept. I am reminded of the words of Paul in the book of Romans who said:

✞

Therefore, I urge you, brothers, in view of God's mercy, to offer your bodies as living sacrifices, holy and pleasing to God—this is your spiritual act of worship. **Romans 12:1**

Paul's concept is that we are to be "living sacrifices" for God. That is, we are to live in positive loving ways that serve God by helping and blessing others. A living sacrifice becomes a "spiritual act of worship."

This concept is directly opposed to the Islamic concept of a "death sacrifice" as the highest deed that can be done for Allah with the greatest reward. The teachings of Islam definitely allow the "martyr" to say "for me to die is paradise!"

بِسْمِ اللهِ الرَّحْمٰنِ الرَّحِيمِ

Seeing The World
With "New Glasses"

> *As cited in Ibn Abbas:*
> *The apes are Jews, the people of the Sabbath;*
> *while the swine are the Christians,*
> *the infidels of the communion of Jesus.*
> Saudi Arabia eighth grade textbook

> *If anyone says, "I love God," yet hates his brother,*
> *he is a liar. For anyone who does not love*
> *his brother, whom he has seen,*
> *cannot love God, whom he has not seen.*
> 1 John 4:20

We have now completed our journey through *The 9/11 Verses*. It is quite powerful to re-read the Koran verses and Hadith passages together without interruption. The Appendix assembles all the Koran verses and Hadith passages together without a break. I highly recommend you read them again to realize their full impact.

As I have mentioned before, until I read the Koran and Hadith, I never knew that these texts existed. This is because for the most part these *9/11 Verses* have remained secret and hidden from the larger public debate. One of the goals of this book is to bring these Koran verses and Hadith stories into the open. I am sure that knowledge of these texts will change the perception of Islam of all who read them, just as it changed mine.

The 9/11 Verses

I have brought these *9/11 Verses* to your attention not only as written and practiced 1400 years ago. I have also shown you example after example of interpretation and practice of these texts by contemporary Muslims.

As I have shown, *The 9/11 Verses* exhibit four major elements that create the violence we see by Muslims. Here is a quick review of these elements. First, they create an attitude of hate towards non-Muslims. Second, they are full of commands to kill non-Muslims. Third, they give commands to force Islamic beliefs on non-Muslims. Fourth, they promise a reward of heaven for violence against non-Muslims.

I have never seen or heard any cable television program, radio talk show or newspaper discuss the teachings that *The 9/11 Verses* contain. Maybe the hosts, guests or reporters have just never taken the time to read them, or they are cautious so as not to scare the public. However it is my belief that the public should be aware.

Mainstream media deliberately hides truth

There are some indications that journalists are making every effort to keep these facts from the public. Dick Morris, in his recently published book, *Fleeced*, uncovered this fact. About one month after 9/11, The Society of Professional Journalists published a set of guidelines for the media in covering the war on terrorism. These guidelines direct reporters to avoid descriptions such as, "Islamic terrorist" or "Muslim extremist" or "Jihad." Instead, they recommend terms like, "Al-Qaeda terrorists" or "political Islamists." the guidelines define "Jihad" as "exerting oneself for the good of Islam and to better oneself." I have shown you the actual scriptures and actions of Muhammad regarding Jihad. The definition they give journalists to use is far from the truth.

As I read through the guidelines, found at www.spj.org/div guidelines.asp, it was apparent that they are trying to downplay the connection between the Islamic religion and terrorism. As I have shown you, the Islamic religion *is* the main reason for terrorism.

Remember this quote from Muhammad I uncovered for you in the chapter called "Live and Let Die?"

Muslim Hadith Book 037, Number 6665:

Abu Musa' reported that Allah's Messenger (may peace be upon him) said: When it will be the Day of Resurrection Allah would deliver to every Muslim a Jew or a Christian and say: That is your rescue from Hell-Fire.

This one quote alone proves my point that this information is being deliberately withheld from you. If a well-know preacher, such as Billy Graham, said that Muslims and Jews were going to be thrown into hell by Jesus to save Christians, how long do you think it would be before every mainstream media news outlet was reporting and condemning his words? If the Christian Bible contained this teaching, the mainstream media would bend over backwards to make sure that every man, women and child in the nation knew it!

The society of professional journalists is an influential organization with 10,000 members and 250 chapters nationwide. The fact that *The 9/11 Verses* are continuing to be kept hidden by journalists shows that these guidelines are being followed. Remember this each time you see a news story on terrorism. What are they trying to hide from you?

Interpretation – depends on what the meaning of "is" is.

Throughout the pages of this book I have given thought to whether I am interpreting correctly the violent verses in the Koran and Muhammad's sayings and actions in the Hadith. When interpreting a text one looks at the meaning of various words, and the context in which they are used. The context can change the meaning of the same words.

For example look at the first words of the hymn "Onward Christian Soldiers."

Onward, Christian soldiers, marching as to war,
with the cross of Jesus going on before!

Christ, the royal Master, leads against the foe;
forward into battle, see, his banners go.

This hymn uses the words "war," "soldiers," "foe" and "battle." These are words that if taken in one context could mean a physical fight with literal killing and violence. In this interpretation, the writer would be describing Christians taking up weapons and marching out to kill their non-Christian enemies.

Taken in another context the same words are symbolic representations of a spiritual war. When the entire hymn is read, it is clear that it is not describing a violent physical battle with Christian soldiers killing non-Christian enemies. Therefore the context of the hymn determines that the meaning of the words "war," "soldiers," "foe" and "battle" are symbolic of a battle that is spiritual not physical.

An examination of the context in the violent verses of the Koran reveals that they mean what they appear to say. The Hadith, which records Muhammad's life and sayings, is clear on how he interpreted the Koran. How can a true Muslim ignore the violent actions of the founder of Islam as well as the verses in the Koran that inspire it?

Even if you believe that all these verses encouraging violence in the Koran and violent actions of Muhammad are misinterpreted, they still exist. Not only do they exist, but volumes of Islamic scholarship over hundreds of years reinforce and strengthen them.

This is enough for Muslim clerics, and schools to be able to preach and incite violence. It really does not matter how you or others interpret Islam. What matters is the "religion of peace" offers enough violent scriptures that anyone who wants to can use them to justify hate, violence and killing.

Saudi Arabia uses them to fill its textbooks for school children with hate against non-Muslims. Nina Shea, in a May 21, 2006 piece entitled, "This is a Saudi Textbook. (After the intolerance was removed.)," found at www.washingtonpost.com, has uncovered modern school textbook teachings that prove this. Here are some excerpts from the article.

FOURTH GRADE

"True belief means ... that you hate the polytheists and infidels but do not treat them unjustly."

FIFTH GRADE

"Whoever obeys the Prophet and accepts the oneness of God cannot maintain a loyal friendship with those who oppose God and His Prophet, even if they are his closest relatives."

"It is forbidden for a Muslim to be a loyal friend to someone who does not believe in God and His Prophet, or someone who fights the religion of Islam."

"A Muslim, even if he lives far away, is your brother in religion. Someone who opposes God, even if he is your brother by family tie, is your enemy in religion."

The 9/11 Verses

EIGHTH GRADE

✠ *"As cited in Ibn Abbas: The apes are Jews, the people of the Sabbath; while the swine are the Christians, the infidels of the communion of Jesus."*

ELEVENTH GRADE

✠ *"The greeting 'Peace be upon you' is specifically for believers. It cannot be said to others." "If one comes to a place where there is a mixture of Muslims and infidels, one should offer a greeting intended for the Muslims."*

✠ *"Do not yield to them [Christians and Jews] on a narrow road out of honor and respect."*

TWELFTH GRADE

✠ *"Jihad in the path of God – which consists of battling against unbelief, oppression, injustice, and those who perpetrate it – is the summit of Islam. This religion arose through jihad and through jihad was its banner raised high. It is one of the noblest acts, which brings one closer to God, and one of the most magnificent acts of obedience to God."*

Saudi textbook writers do not make this stuff up out of thin air. They get their ideas from the verses in the Koran and the passages in the Hadith. These teachings echo the verses and passages that I have disclosed in this book. The Muslim violence equation is clearly at work in these textbooks. Children are taught attitudes of hate towards non-Muslims, and glorification of holy war. Is it any wonder that most of the 9/11 hijackers were Saudi Arabian?

A new pair of glasses

Reading the Koran and Hadith is like putting on a new pair of glasses with which to view the world. In the aftermath of 9/11 we were deluged with explanations for the actions of the Muslims who carried out the attacks.

We were told that the cause was economic. We were told that the west was at fault. We should talk with them. We should listen to them and try and understand. Our support for Israel was to blame. Some commentators urged Americans to be more understanding and tolerant of Islam. Others opined that the terrorists attacked because we had invaded "Muslim lands." A few pundits theorized Muslims were paying us back for all the Iraqi children that supposedly died because of sanctions against Iraq.

All of these explanations ignore the plain and simple truth of the violent teachings of Islam. Is it not much more likely that Islam itself is the cause of 9/11 and all other acts of Muslim violence?

Equipped with this direct knowledge of *The 9/11 Verses* one can understand and interpret the world of Islam and its interaction with the non-Muslim world in a new light. I now know how to understand news stories involving Islamic terrorism. When I read the quotes and statements from Muslims involved in violence, I see in them the passages of the Koran and Hadith.

While knowledge and understanding of this part of the Islamic Religion may not be pleasant, it is better to be aware of the danger than to remain ignorant.

Now, with my "new glasses" firmly in place, let me give you some of my thoughts on Islam in relation to some key topics for our time.

A religion of peace?

Take a look at the following four statements, found on www.beliefnet.com, and made by Muslims regarding the idea of whether hate and violence against non-Muslims is part of Islam. I have underlined those parts of the statements that I found particularly interesting in light of what we have discovered in *The 9/11 Verses*.

Islam stresses public order and the rule of law. Terrorism destroys this social order and decreases the tranquility of life that Islam emphasizes. During the life of <u>the Prophet Muhammad,</u> whenever there was a choice between conflict and social order, he <u>always chose the path of least violence unless forced to do otherwise.</u> The Qur'an [Koran] has a strong ethical orientation to help people regardless of their religious affiliation and <u>calls people to faith based on reason and spiritual intuition, not force.</u> Terrorism is an imposition of force and fear to change the minds of people. Muslims must show non-Muslims the beauty of our religion, create peace between peoples, and promote justice and the rule of law. Terrorism runs counter to all these values, and therefore absolutely goes against Islam.

Shahed Amanullah
<u>www.beliefnet.com/gallery/terrorist.html</u>

Americans should turn off the TV and look for opportunities to get to know their Muslim neighbor because it will alleviate a great deal of fear and anxiety. The most important teachings of the Prophet Muhammad (peace be upon him) on this issue are about the rights of the neighbor, and that <u>the neighbor has rights on a Muslim that are almost as strong as the rights of family. No one can be called a true believer if his neighbor, or anyone in his community, is afraid of him</u> — these are the guiding principles for the vast majority of Muslims. It's these teachings that make those Muslims want to be good citizens and good friends to those people around. _Terrorism isn't part of our religion, and never has been._

Dr. Ingrid Mattson
www.beliefnet.com/gallery/terrorist.html

The Holy Qur'an [Koran] teaches us that "Whoever kills a human being ... it is as if he has killed all humankind; and if he saves a human life, it is as if he has saved the lives of all humankind (Qur'an 5:32)." _Islam condemns the abuse of religion by fanatics whose purpose is to rouse hate and beget further violence._ Nothing is as antithetical to all religion as when wanton violence is wreaked by extremists. Millions of Muslims live in peace with the world around them. They are examples of Islam's true harmony and are fighting against terrorism through dialogue, knowledge, and outreach. And _the Prophet of Islam serves as the ultimate example of compassion and love to Muslims._ So to sink to violence against innocents serves no purpose in Islam.

Imam Abdul Feisal Rauf
www.beliefnet.com/gallery/terrorist.html

I get clarity about what Islam can be through the fact that one of Allah's 99 names is Al-Wadud, or ... 'The Loving One.' While it's easy to demonize Islam based on the actions of extremists, in reality _our faith is founded on progressive principles of tolerance and inclusion._ In a book of mine I offered "99 Precepts for Opening Hearts, Minds and Doors in the Muslim World" inspired by Allah's names. The first precept—live with an open heart to others—is based on the name Al-Wadud. _What sets apart the American Muslim experience is we can stand up to extremists without fearing violent retaliation from the fanatical Muslims we oppose._

The 9/11 Verses

With this freedom, we must continue to speak out against those who commit acts of terror in the name of Islam.

Asra Q. Nomani
www.beliefnet.com/gallery/terrorist.html

Here are the excerpts from the four statements all in one place.

- ...the Prophet Muhammad, ...always chose the path of least violence unless forced to do otherwise.

- ...The Qur'an ...calls people to faith based on reason and spiritual intuition, not force.

- ...the neighbor has rights on a Muslim that are almost as strong as the rights of family. No one can be called a true believer if his neighbor, or anyone in his community, is afraid of him...

- Terrorism isn't part of our religion, and never has been.

- Islam condemns the abuse of religion by fanatics whose purpose is to rouse hate and beget further violence.

- ...the Prophet of Islam serves as the ultimate example of compassion and love to Muslims.

- ...our faith is founded on progressive principles of tolerance and inclusion.

After reading the verses from the Koran and the passages from the life of Muhammad, can you say that these quotes make any sense at all?

Freedom and Islam

Can freedom as we know it in the western world exist side by side with Islam? In this great country individuals are free to choose the faith that they believe they should practice. Citizens in free countries are able to read books that contain varied opinions and ideas in matters of thought and faith.

Freedom in matters of conscience and faith means that no government agency, police force, or private organization, can force me to think and act against my own beliefs. The constitution of the United States protects the free exercise of religious faith. Private churches and other private institutions can set down doctrines and standards of behavior. However, individuals are free to leave those churches and institutions should they find irreconcilable differences. They can leave without the fear of being killed as Muhammad directed for being apostate .

Freedom, as we know it today, allows individuals to do and say things that a faith or government group might find offensive. If I can believe and say that Muhammad was a false prophet who did not speak truth about God, then, I am free. When I am able to criticize the president of the United States and call for new policies, I am free. Muslims may not like what I believe and say about their prophet, but freedom means I can say it. The president of the United States may think that I am wrong in my complaints, but freedom means I can complain.

Freedom not only allows me to hold my own beliefs, but I can debate and persuade others in an attempt to get them to change their beliefs. If I am a conservative, I can discuss ideas with liberals to get them to change their minds. As a Christian, I can explain and debate my faith with Muslims and try and lead them to Christ. Likewise Muslims can preach their faith to Christians to persuade them to become Muslim.

Freedom involves the free and open exchange of thoughts and ideas. This exchange takes place in personal conversations, books, newspapers, magazines, classrooms, radio, television and movies. This process goes on without threats of force to keep thoughts and ideas from being expressed.

Can anyone honestly believe that the Islamic Religion welcomes the free and open exchange of thoughts and ideas? In countries, where Muslims are the majority, is freedom of conscience and faith allowed? I have gone over example after example of these freedoms being denied in countries with majority Muslim populations.

I have discussed the fact that Islam has rules and regulations for many of the details of life. I have shown you very few of these parts of the Koran and Hadith, but they are worth mentioning here in the context of freedom. In Islamic countries, where the faith is taken seriously, personal freedoms are sharply curtailed.

The ultimate freedom is the freedom to worship God as you see fit. Once you have become Muslim, it is strictly forbidden for you to leave the faith. If you decide to leave, you are an apostate and must be killed according to the messenger of Allah. This is a denial of the freedom of worship.

Being able to speak your mind even if it offends others is a key part of freedom. Islam requires that anyone who insults Allah or Muhammad should be killed. This is denial of the freedom of thought and speech as well as legitimizing murder.

The practice of Islam takes various forms in different countries. There are Muslims who ignore the prophet and Koran verses and practice an Islam that allows individual freedom. But they are not practicing true Islam. Muhammad shows us what true Islam is like. Freedom as we know in the western world cannot exist side by side with the faith of the prophet.

Slavery and Islam

Freedom also means not being owned by another. The issue of slavery is one where the Koran and Muhammad are firmly against freedom. Muhammad himself owned slaves. Allah in the Koran gives the stamp of approval on slavery. Not only is slavery given divine approval but also the rape of slave girls is given the green light.

Happy now the believers... who restrain their appetites, (save with their wives, or the slaves whom their right hands possess): for in that case they shall be free from blame...

The Koran, Chapter 23:1-5

This Koran verse gives approval to possess slave girls and enjoy them sexually. Since a slave has no free choice in the matter, sex with them is clearly rape. Allah legitimizes rape. Muhammad approved of slavery having owned slaves himself. He also approved of the rape of women captured as slaves in his wars.

Bukhari Hadith Volume 5, Book 59, Number 459
Narrated by Ibn Muhairiz

I entered the Mosque and saw Abu Said Al-Khudri and sat beside him and asked him about Al-Azl (i.e. coitus interruptus). Abu Said said, "We went out with Allah's Apostle for the Ghazwa of Banu Al-Mustaliq and we received captives from among the Arab captives and we desired women and celibacy became hard on us and we loved to do coitus interruptus. So when we intended to do coitus interruptus, we said, 'How can we do coitus interruptus before asking Allah's Apostle who is present among us?' We asked (him) about it and he said, 'It is better for you not to do so, for if any soul (till the Day of Resurrection) is predestined to exist, it will exist.' "

Muhammad could have condemned the practice of slavery and the rape of slaves but instead tells his followers that it is better that they do not practice "coitus interruptus." His men did this so the slaves would not become pregnant. Pregnant slaves could not be sold for as much.

In 1961, Sean O'Callahan published a book entitled *The Slave Trade Today*. The book describes what he saw on his tour of the slave trade markets in Africa and the Mideast. Here is how he described one slave market in Saudi Arabia.

"I was awakened by shouts and screams coming from the courtyard. Rushing to the window I looked down to see a dozen slaves being herded through a door at the far end of the yard. They were being driven in like cattle by three hefty guards armed with long lashed whips. Even as I watched, one of the poor wretches, a Sudanese girl with huge breasts, received a savage lash across her naked buttocks let out a shriek of agony.

"As the next slave was led in, a murmur of excitement went up among the buyers and they crowded closer around the rostrum. He was a slender boy of about 12 years old with beautiful classical Arab features. Although much has been written about Arab brotherhood and solidarity, I knew that the Arab has no compunction in enslaving his fellows should they fall into his hands.

"The boy was naked and tried to cover his privates with his little hands and he ran up the steps of the rostrum....there is an age old saying among the Bedouin: 'A goat for use, a girl for enjoyment, but a boy for ecstasy.' He (the now purchased slave

150

boy) was claimed by a tall bearded Arab who led him from the
rostrum with an arm around his waist."

Islam does provide for regulation of slavery and tells its followers to treat their slaves "justly." But the faith approves of owning humans and treating them like property. Saudi Arabia officially outlawed slavery in 1962. Most Muslim countries have done likewise. However all indications are that slavery still exists in the Muslim world but keeps a low profile. Enforcement of the laws against slavery is rare. It has been found that Muslims have even acted as slave owners in the United States. Here are some excerpts from a September 1, 2006 article entitled "Saudi Gets 27 Years to Life for Enslaving Maid" by Barbara Ferguson, found at www.arabnews.com.

WASHINGTON, 1 September 2006 A Saudi man convicted of sexually assaulting an Indonesian housekeeper and keeping her as a virtual slave was sentenced yesterday to 27 years to life in prison in Colorado.

Homaidan Al-Turki, the 37-year-old Saudi national, denied the charges and blamed anti-Muslim prejudice for the case against him. He said prosecutors persuaded the housekeeper to accuse him after they failed to build a case that he was a terrorist.

Al-Turki, who was studying for a doctoral degree at the University of Colorado, was convicted June 30 of unlawful sexual contact by use of force, theft and extortion. All are felonies.

He was also convicted on misdemeanor counts of false imprisonment and conspiracy to commit false imprisonment.

After the judge denied a motion for a new trial yesterday, defense attorney John Richilano said he would appeal the convictions. The lawyer argued that cultural differences were at the heart of the charges.

Al-Turki said he treated the woman the same way any observant Muslim family would treat a daughter. "Your honor, I am not here to apologize, for I cannot apologize for things I did not do and for crimes I did not commit," he told the judge. "The state has criminalized these basic Muslim behaviors. Attacking traditional Muslim behaviors was the focal point of the prosecution."

This Saudi man, in line with Islam's teaching, had no problem with treating his "maid" like property and using her sexually. Thankfully this country has criminalized these types of "basic Muslim behaviors."

The "Christian world" has had its problems with slavery. However Christianity never made slavery a doctrine of the faith. Certainly there were no revelations from God or practices from the life of Jesus that blessed the institution of owning people as property and/or using them sexually.

Christianity teaches that mankind is in slavery and bondage to sin. Christ has come to set us free from this slavery to sin. Freedom is a strong positive concept in the faith. That is in part why Christians have succeeded in fighting against and eliminating slavery in most areas of the world. In fact, Christians have been on the forefront of every major political battle to outlaw slavery.

Democracy and Islam

Is democracy compatible with Islam? Freedom house detailed the state of democracy in the countries of the world in a study released in December 18, 2001. They found that Islamic states were three times less likely to be democratic than non-Islamic states. This means that only 23 percent of states with an Islamic majority were democratic. In contrast 75 percent of states where Muslims are in the minority are electoral democracies.

Democracy has been on the rise in the world over the last two decades. Every region of the world over this time has seen major increases in democracy. This is not true for countries with majority Muslim populations.

There are 192 countries in the world. Countries that are considered not free number 48. Almost 60 percent of the not-free countries have populations that are a majority Muslim. Countries that are not free withhold a broad range of political, economic and religious freedoms from their populations.

Democracy provides a framework by which citizens can change their government, if need be. This includes changing the laws under which these citizens must live. The ability to change laws allows flexibility in how civilized society is organized. The opportunity to change laws also allows for the correction of past mistakes and injustices. For example, at one time slavery was legal in the United States and that was a terrible wrong. The laws allowing and promoting slavery were not divine rules fixed in stone, and so could be changed.

I have shown that when Islam is taken seriously there is no separation of church and state. So the laws of the state under Islamic law become very rigid and, for all practical purposes, fixed. The ability of citizens in an Islamic state to change laws is sharply diminished. Islamic law is akin to a very detailed constitution that allows little change. Since these are the laws of Allah himself, they should be obeyed and not changed or questioned.

Saudi Arabia, a strict Islamic state, is a good example. Women are not allowed to drive cars. There is talk of changing this law. Changing this law is possible because the Koran and Hadith are silent on this matter. Women are also not allowed out in public without a male relative. This law is part of the Koran and Hadith and so cannot be changed. Pork and alcohol are illegal since the

Koran outlaws them. There is no room for changing this law since Allah has clearly ruled on the matter.

Another important feature in western democracy is the protection and balancing of the rights of minorities with that of majorities. Without this, democracy can become mob rule with the powerful majority taking advantage of those who are weaker and smaller in number.

I have shown that non-Muslims are treated like second class citizens in the doctrines, laws and Holy Writings of Islam. Islam is a direct revelation from Allah on how everyone should live. Islam is superior. Islam is correct. So Islam does not need to make any accommodations for other beliefs. When Islam rules, non-Muslim minorities suffer.

Democracy can be practiced within the framework of Islam. But where the faith is taken seriously (such as Saudi Arabia and Iran) democracy takes place within the narrow confines of the detailed divine and unchangeable Islamic law.

This type of "democracy" is not anything like the one we in the western world know and practice. Western style democracy is definitely not compatible with Islam.

Nuclear weapons and Islam

Now that you have your "new pair of glasses," what do you see when you look at the issue of nuclear weapons in the hands of an Islamic state? Or what about a nuclear weapon or two in the hands of committed followers of Muhammad who take his example of violence seriously? This book has shown that true followers of Islam do not think and act in ways that I would consider civilized and rational.

For many years the Soviet Union and the United States stood poised to deliver thousand of nuclear bombs to each other's homelands. During the Cuban missile crises we came very close to nuclear war. But war never happened. This is because of the doctrine of Mutually Assured Destruction.

MAD, as the doctrine is aptly acronymed, said that any nuclear war between the two rival powers would have resulted in both countries being damaged to such a degree that they are essentially destroyed. MAD acted as a deterrent that prevented either side from starting a nuclear war. The leaders of both the Soviet Union and the United States knew if they did, both countries would be destroyed.

MAD assumes a certain commonality of goals and interests between the leaders of the rival countries. Like Islam, communism seeks to expand and dominate the whole earth. However as an atheistic system, communism believes this world is all there is. So it would serve no rational purpose for communism to start a war in which it is destroyed along with its enemies. Additionally under communist beliefs there is no reward in the after life for actions taken here on earth.

Those who follow the Koran verses and the Hadith disclosed in this book would not hesitate to use nuclear weapons to destroy non-Muslims. It would not matter that they in turn would be destroyed. To them it would be no different than the suicide bomber who offers his life for Allah as he kills infidels.

In fact, due to the massive scale of the destruction, would not the use of nuclear weapons please Allah all the more? Massive killing of non-believers for Allah, caused by the use of a nuclear bomb, would surely, in the Islamic mind of the bomber, result in massive rewards for him and his family. Perhaps he would gain thousands of lusty virgins instead of just the few promised to your run of the mill Islamic killer.

Modern technology gives Islam the ability to destroy infidels on a scale that is unimaginable. Nuclear bombs and other weapons of mass destruction in the hands of committed Muslims are all the more dangerous in today's world.

Parts of Muhammad's example are not harmonious with contemporary society

As a Christian, I have studied the life of Christ. There is absolutely nothing he did or said that is not compatible with twenty first-century modern day life and sensibilities. In fact the history of the civilized world's moral development has seen a consistent march in the direction of the ideals exhibited by the life and words of Christ.

The rules and laws that our modern societies function under are in the spirit of what Christ taught. Jesus's teachings of fairness, justice, equality, forgiveness, and love are ideals that all good people aspire to.

There is much in the life of Muhammad that is in conflict with twenty first century modern day life and sensibilities. This is a huge problem because Islam teaches that the things Muhammad did and what he approved and disapproved of is the divine law of Allah. The prophet is held up as a holy and righteous example for the world. The Koran calls Muhammad a "noble pattern." "Noble" means that he is of a high and excellent moral character. "Pattern" means the prophet is a model for us that is worthy of imitation.

Muhammed at age 51 married a six year old little girl named A'isha. She lived with her parents until age nine. At this time Muhammad, now 54, consummated the marriage by having sex with A'isha then a pre-pubescent nine year old girl. The age of marriage in certain Muslim countries is set at nine. This is because the lawmakers believe that what the messenger of Allah did is the law and will of God and should be imitated. Muhammad approved of owning other human beings as property. The prophet had sex with his slave girls and approved of others doing so also with their own slave girls.

As you know when the prophet would win battles they would kill the men and divide up the women for sexual purposes. After the victory in a battle against the Jews of Khaibar, one of Muhammad's jihadists asked for a slave girl for his sexual use. The prophet told the man to choose any girl he wanted. Later, Muhammad learned that his soldier had picked the most beautiful girl. When the prophet saw for himself her stunning beauty he took her away from his warrior and told him to choose another girl. Thus the prophet did not keep his word.

The Hadith records another incident between the prophet and his adopted son's wife. Muhammad went to his son's house one day and saw his sons wife scantily clad and told those he was with that she had great beauty. The woman overheard the comment. This set in motion events that ended with the prophets adopted son divorcing his wife so that Muhammad could marry her. Muhammad told him not to divorce her but he did anyway and the prophet married her.

The separation of man and wife that a Jihad creates can make a man very lustful. So to satisfy this lust, Muhammad instituted a "temporary" marriage. This form of divine sanctioned prostitution allowed his men to satisfy their sexual lusts at will. Here is the Hadith passage about this.

Bukhari Hadith Volume 6, Book 60, Number 139
Narrated by Abdullah Ibn Abbas

We used to participate in the holy wars carried on by the Prophet and we had no women (wives) with us. So we said (to the Prophet). "Shall we castrate ourselves?" But the Prophet forbade us to do that and thenceforth he allowed us to marry a woman (temporarily) by giving her even a garment, and then he recited: "O you who believe! Do not make unlawful the good things which Allah has made lawful for you."

The 9/11 Verses

Modern day Muslims practice the prophets teaching on temporary marriage. Here are some excerpts from a January 20, 2007 article entitled "Temporary 'Enjoyment Marriages' In Vogue Again With Some Iraqis" found at www.washingtonpost.com.

BAGHDAD — Fatima Ali was a 24-year-old divorcee with no high school diploma and no job. Shawket al-Rubae was a 34-year-old Shiite sheik with a pregnant wife who, he said, could not have sex with him. Ali wanted someone to take care of her. Rubae wanted a companion.

They met one afternoon in May at the house he shares with his wife, in the room where he accepts visitors seeking his religious counsel. He had a proposal. Would Ali be his temporary wife? He would pay her 5,000 Iraqi dinars up front — about $4 — in addition to her monthly expenses. About twice a week over the next eight months, he would summon her to a house he would rent.

The negotiations took an hour and ended with an unwritten agreement, the couple recalled. Thus began their "mutaa," or enjoyment marriage, a temporary union believed by Shiite Muslims to be sanctioned by Islamic law. The Shiite practice began 1,400 years ago, in what is now Iraq and other parts of the region, as a way to provide for war widows. Banned by President Saddam Hussein's Sunni-led government, it has regained popularity since the 2003 U.S.-led invasion of Iraq brought the majority Shiites to power, said clerics, women's rights activists and mutaa spouses.

According to Shiite religious law, a mutaa relationship can last for a few minutes or several years. A man can have an unlimited number of mutaa wives and a permanent wife at the same time. A woman can have only one husband at a time, permanent or temporary. No written contract or official ceremony is required in a mutaa. When the time limit ends, the man and woman go their separate ways with none of the messiness of a regular divorce.

The article says that the practice of temporary marriage began as a way to "provide for war widows." The quote that I have shown you from the Hadith demonstrates that the practice was started to provide Allah sanctioned sex for lusting Jihad warriors. This article is again an example of the fact that Islamic verses and passages are hidden from the public.

The article goes on to detail objections to the practice from within the Islamic community. Many Sunni Arabs believe that the mutaa wives are being exploited because they are poor. Women's rights activists believe that the practice is plain and simple another name for religiously sanctioned prostitution. They see the practice as taking Iraq backwards from modern times and away from democracy.

Those that defend the practice say that it keeps young women from having sexual relations out of wedlock. They also assert that the difference between mutaa marriage and traditional marriage is not that great. A cleric named Mahdi al-Shog asserted that the practice of temporary marriage was created for the purpose of helping women.

It may be true that the practice was justified as a help to war widows. However it should be considered that in many cases the "war widows" that the jihad warriors were "helping" were made widows because Muhammad's men killed their husbands.

The practice is obviously a "help" to men. Men can have as many women as will agree to the temporary marriage. The "marriage" can last for just a few minutes. Women cannot participate in this sexual bonanza as they are only allowed one relationship at a time. It is clear that this practice is fundamentally based on fulfilling the sexual lusts of men.

Islamic "marriage" in this context is a very low view of the purpose of a man and women joining together in matrimony. The Christian faith takes a high view of marriage. Christians believe that husband and wife become "one flesh" when they join together in marriage. The Bible commands married couples to "keep the marriage bed undefiled." This means that extramarital sexual experiences are not to be a part of a marriage. Therefore a Christian man is not to join himself with a prostitute or any other women under any circumstances.

Marriage in the Christian context is an example of Christ's relationship to the church. The church is said to be the "bride of Christ." Christ is faithful to the church. A Christian man should likewise be faithful to his wife.

To follow the "noble pattern" of the prophet in these matters would require that our twenty first-century society give up the moral progress we have made in these areas. How many parents would want the United States to legalize marriage down to the age of nine? Should we likewise revert back to the days of slavery and allow the use of human beings as sexual toys? Must we degrade the entire concept of marriage by allowing "Mutaa" relationships for men? The prophet ordered the killing of homosexuals. Should our law be changed to follow this rule of Allah as relayed by Muhammad?

Moderate Muslims

There are Muslims who are peaceful. Perhaps even a majority of them are. Of course that is hard to tell since most Muslims live in countries where they are by far the majority of the population. In fact 72 percent of Muslims live in countries where the Muslim population exceeds 70 percent. So they are surrounded by culture and laws that conform for the most part to what they believe.

It is possible that Muslims in their daily lives are at peace, since their neighbors are as they are. They do not have to make a lot of choices on how they interact with infidels since non-Muslims are so few and far between.

The Muslim population in the United States seems to have taken, for the greater part, the path of peaceful living with those who are not Muslim. However at only three-point-five percent of the population, they would not stand a chance in a fight. Even Muhammad was peaceful in his early years when his followers were few. As he gained numbers and power the violence began.

Most of the U.S. Muslims remain moderate by choosing to ignore the violent verses and passages in the Holy Writings of Islam. In faith and practice they follow the tolerant portions of the Koran.

Most Muslims do not kill unbelievers for Allah. But almost all who kill others in the name of God are Muslim. Most Muslims are average people going about their daily lives just like people of other faiths.

Does moderate Islam exist? By moderate, I mean does their faith have the ability to peacefully co-exist with those of us in the world that are not Muslim? Can Islam treat those outside it as equals?

Islam is not a moderate faith. However, many Muslims are moderate and live and let live with other faiths. It is my opinion that these Muslims are not practicing Islam the way it is taught in the Koran and Hadith.

The Koran and Muhammad teach that Islam will reign supreme and one day be the only faith on the earth. Those who kill for Allah believe they are helping to make this happen here and now during our time in history. The rest of the Muslims still believe that Islam will be supreme, but are not doing anything to force it to happen. These Muslims believe it will happen sometime way in the distant future long after they are dead and gone.

There are two types of moderate Muslims. First, there are those who refuse to practice the violent parts of the faith and are working to reform Islam. The second, are those who ignore the violent parts of Islam and practice only the peaceful portions, while being respectful and tolerant to those of other faiths.

Moderate Muslims who want to reform Islam

There are moderate Muslims who are leading reform movements within Islam. One such movement is called "Muslims against Sharia." You can find them at www.reformislam.org. Sharia law is civil and criminal law derived from Islamic writings. Countries under Sharia law have completely merged church and state. As I have discussed before, Muslims against Sharia seek to remove verses from the Koran that promote hatred and violence. As an alternative, the violence promoting verses could be declared invalid. They would then be marked so readers will know which revelations they should ignore.

On their website, Muslims against Sharia provides a list of all the verses they would like to remove from Islam. Here are some excerpts of their manifesto.

Acknowledging mistakes

The majority of the terrorist acts of the last three decades, including the 9/11 attacks, were perpetrated by Islamic fundamentalists in the name of Islam. We, as Muslims, find it abhorrent that Islam is used to murder millions of innocent people, Muslims and non-Muslims alike.

Inconsistencies in the Koran

Unfortunately, Islamic religious texts, including the Koran and the Hadith contain many passages, which call

162

for Islamic domination and incite violence against non-Muslims. It is time to change that. Muslim fundamentalists believe that the Koran is the literal word of Allah. But could Allah, the most Merciful, the most Compassionate, command mass slaughter of people whose only fault is being non-Muslim?

✠ The Koran & the Bible

Many Bible figures from Adam to Jesus (Isa) are considered to be prophets and are respected by Islam. Islamic scholars however believe that both the Old and the New Testament came from God, but that they were corrupted by the Jews and Christians over time. While neither Testament calls for mass murder of unbelievers, the Koran does. Could it be possible that the Koran itself was corrupted by Muslims over the last thirteen centuries?

✠ The need for reform

Islam, in its present form, is not compatible with principles of freedom and democracy. Twenty-first century Muslims have two options: we can continue the barbaric policies of the seventh century perpetuated by Hassan al-Banna, Abdullah Azzam, Yassir Arafat, Ruhollah Khomeini, Osama bin Laden, Muslim Brotherhood, al-Qaeda, Hizballah, Hamas, Hizb-ut-Tahrir, etc., leading to a global war between Dar al-Islam (Islamic World) and Dar al-Harb (non-Islamic World), or we can reform Islam to keep our rich cultural heritage and to cleanse our religion from the reviled relics of the past.

We, as Muslims who desire to live in harmony with people of other religions, agnostics, and atheists choose the latter option. We can no longer allow Islamic extremists to use our religion as a weapon. We must protect future

163

generations of Muslims from being brainwashed by the Islamic radicals. If we do not stop the spread of Islamic fundamentalism, our children will become homicidal zombies.

✷ Accepting responsibilities

To start the healing process, we must acknowledge evils done by Muslims in the name of Islam and accept responsibility for those evils. We must remove evil passages from Islamic religious texts, so that future generations of Muslims will not be confused by conflicting messages. Our religious message should be loud and clear: Islam is peace; Islam is love; Islam is light. War, murder, violence, divisiveness and discrimination are not Islamic values.

✷ Religious privacy

Religion is the private matter of every individual. Any person should be able to freely practice any religion as long as the practice does not interfere with the local laws, and no person must be forced to practice any religion. Just as people are created equal, there is no one religion that is superior to another. Any set of beliefs that is spread by force is fundamentally immoral; it is no longer a religion, but a political ideology.

In other words these reformists want to change the Muslim violence equation. I think they have rightly identified the problems with Islam. They have correctly figured out that these *9/11 Verses* in the Koran have lead to massive amounts of violence by Muslims against non-Muslims.

Within the Muslims against Sharia manifesto, is an acknowledgment of the truth of my Muslim violence equation. That is, the

Holy Writings of Islam, as they are today, support a hateful attitude and killing or violence against non-believers.

If they are able to attain their goals, Islam would truly become a religion of peace.

Moderate Muslims who ignore parts of Islam

This group of moderate Muslims are those who ignore the hateful and violent parts of Islam. They choose to believe and practice the tolerant parts of the Koran and Hadith. These are well meaning people who want to live at peace with the non-believers around them.

Christine Huda Dodge wrote a book called *The Everything®* *Understanding Islam Book*. Her book is a prime example of a Muslim choosing to believe the tolerant verses and ignore the violent ones. In her book you will not find any of the violent passages that we uncover for you in this book. She does not acknowledge that they exist, let alone try to explain them. Maybe that is because there is no good way to explain them.

Here is a quote from page 120 of her book that illustrates my point.

The Qur'an does describe the punishment that those who reject faith will face in the Hereafter. However, Muslims are never encouraged to randomly or systematically punish, wage war against, or kill people simply because they do not believe in the message of Islam. Such behavior would be the antithesis of the Qur'anic injunction: "Let there be no compulsion in religion." (2:256)

The Qur'an gives clear instructions to Muslims on how they should interact with those who do not believe, in a chapter of the Qur'an aptly titled Al-Kafiroon (Those Who Reject Faith): "Say: 'Oh you who reject faith! I do not worship what you worship, and you will not worship what I worship. And I will never worship that which you worship, nor will you ever worship that which I worship. You have your faith, and I have mine'" (109:1-6)

These are interpretations of Islamic teachings in regards to force and violence by a moderate Muslim with verses from the Koran to back them up. However ignoring the violent verses and portraying Islam without them is dishonest. The same Koran Ms. Dodge quotes from also says:

Make war upon such of those to whom the Scriptures have been given as believe not in Allah, or in the Last Day, and who forbid not that which Allah and His Apostle have forbidden, and who profess not the profession of truth, until they pay tribute out of hand, and they be humbled.

The Koran, Chapter 9:29

This group of moderate Muslims is probably the largest. They are good people who are sincerely striving to worship as they believe they should. Their daily practice of faith is peaceful and respectful. Their version of Islam is in practice a truly peaceful religion.

The future of Islam

In the coming years, it will be interesting to watch what becomes of the Muslim world. For hundreds of years most Muslims have been born, lived and died in closed societies. Literacy was low especially for women. There was little or no opportunity to see what the world outside the community of Islam was like. Like life under communism, information and ideas were strictly controlled.

Islam, up until the present day, maintains itself mostly by cultural intimidation and the threat of force. In most areas of the world the faith does not allow for the free exchange of ideas.

The world today has changed drastically. The force behind this change is modern technology. Foremost of this technological revolution is the Internet. The Internet allows a free exchange of thought and ideas. A Muslim can sit at a computer and ask questions that he would not dare ask the local Imam. Questions can be asked and answers explored without fear of being punished or killed.

Internet access in the Muslim world is rapidly increasing although it is still low. Some Muslim countries have attempted to restrict access by blocking certain content at the Internet service provider level. The information superhighway allows Muslims to interact with non-Muslims in a way that was never before possible.

I believe that the power that Islam maintains over its people will be drastically reduced in the coming years. This will happen as the claims of Islam are increasingly scrutinized under the microscope of the World Wide Web. Wolfgang Bruno, a European author, says that Islam is a "dinosaur in the age of mammals." He believes that the rational criticism made possible by the Internet will slowly wear Islam down.

This may be true, but much depends on what the worlds one-billion-plus Muslims decide to do with their faith. Will they in faith and practice ignore *The 9/11 Verses* and instead live by the peaceful verses?

Some thoughts from someone who lived under Islam

This is a blog that I found from a man who has lived in an Islamic country. It is hard for us who are used to living free to comprehend what it is like to live under Islam taken seriously.

Basharee Mortadd
March 20th, 2007
www.Faithfreedom.org

… Which brings me to the second reason why I'm blogging: I want to save the product of Judeo-Christian reform called the West. Many of those born into the West do not appreciate what it means to be born with free will, with guaranteed free speech, and with a separation of the church and state. Coming from the hellhole of Islam, I do, and I intend to preserve it. I will not allow my children to go through the psychological hell Islamic nations are going through. I will not allow it for your children.

Islam is a dangerous political ideology that separates the world into 'us' versus 'them,' into Muslim versus kafir, into Dar Al-Islam versus Dar Al-Harb. If there is anything I want you to learn from this boring rant, it's this: Muslims cannot coexist in peace with non-Muslims. Muslims hate you and will never be pleased with you unless you're a living Muslim, a humiliated dhimmi, or a dead infidel.

Mr. Mortadd is in effect calling all of us in the west to open our eyes to the truth about Islam. I know my eyes are now open, and I hope *The 9/11 Verses* have opened yours. I find it encouraging that someone like Mr. Mortadd can come out of that situation and be so appreciative of the blessings that we in the west take so for granted.

168

A hope for the future

In the coming years, when you see continued violence by Muslims around the world, remember *The 9/11 Verses* you have learned here. For the foreseeable future there will be those who take Islam seriously and will follow the "noble pattern" of violence in the Koran and Hadith. The question is how much influence these faithful will have over the totality of what is Islam.

After learning these unpleasant facts about Islam, it would be easy to despair about the future relations between the non-Islamic and Islamic worlds. However, I am not in despair and I believe there are reasons to be hopeful.

Modern communication and technology will help

With modern communication technology rapidly spreading across the globe, the days of closed societies are coming to an end. This communication revolution will continue to bring religious and political ideas out in the open for all to see. This will help people to make truly informed choices in matters of faith and practice.

Closed non-democratic systems are at a disadvantage in our modern technologically driven world. They cannot keep up with the free worlds ability, through capitalism and free markets, to provide opportunity for people to grow and improve themselves. Non-free market societies are also unable to sustain themselves militarily compared to their counterparts.

When I was in college in the late seventies and early eighties, there was constant talk about possible war with the Soviet Union. During this time the Reagan administration began a multi-year program to build up the United States military forces. At that time, the USSR looked strong and powerful. In November 1989, just a few years later, the Berlin wall came crashing down. By December 1991, The Union of Soviet Socialist Republics was no more. The handicap of poor economics, caused by a non-capitalistic closed society, forced its collapse. Without a good economy the Soviet Union did not have the resources to match the US military might.

Our military is strong, but our resolve must be stronger

In terms of military might there will not be any threat from the Islamic world that cannot be met and overcome by the free world. However, this will require the free world to not back down in the face of Islamic aggression.

All of us need to understand that those Muslims, who believe in *The 9/11 Verses*, and have dedicated their lives to living by their precepts, cannot be reasoned with. No amount of diplomacy or negotiation will change people like Osama Bin Laden. Like millions of other terrorists, Osama is a true believer in *The 9/11 Verses*. The only way to deal with true believers is to totally defeat them.

Those who control the mainstream media have taken the path of downplaying and covering up the truth of the role of *The 9/11 Verses* in this conflict. They think that by appeasing violent Islam, that somehow, we will "all just get along." All of you who have read this book know better.

We should not allow intolerant Islam to expand

In Europe, many Muslims are increasingly trying to set up their own Islamic states within the western countries in which they reside. They want to set up separate court systems to dispense Islamic justice within their communities. We need to elect leaders who will not allow this to happen. As you have seen, Islam is a system that is extremely intolerant of the beliefs of others. We should not allow Muslims to expand intolerant systems of thought and justice into our society.

Some European countries have allowed large numbers of Muslim immigrants to enter their countries. As the percent of the population that is Muslim grows, so have problems associated with Islamic intolerance. Countries should stop allowing large numbers of people that subscribe to hate and intolerance to immigrate. Diversity does not always enrich a society. Sometimes it degrades and reduces the quality of our lives.

France has appropriately not allowed Muslim girls to wear the Islamic clothing when in public schools. The United Kingdom has shut down Mosques where *The 9/11 Verses* have been taught and violence against British citizens has been advocated. Free speech is important. But being alive to enjoy the right of free speech is also important.

Muslims and ex-Muslims offer support

I am encouraged also by comments from Muslims and ex-Muslims who have rejected the violent parts of Islam. They are supplying the debate with their experiences and thoughts about violence and Islam. This will be a positive influence on current and future generations as the youth of the world contemplate what causes to dedicate their lives to.

Ex-Muslims, having lived in the culture produced by *The 9/11 Verses*, can teach others from their experiences. They have helped others extricate themselves from the web of hate that fuels terrorist acts.

Muslims who are trying to reform Islam have a tough task ahead of them. It is unclear to me how they can accomplish their goals when they are dealing with a faith that firmly believes in the divine inspiration of *The 9/11 Verses*. However, I support and applaud their efforts.

Love is more powerful than hate

As a Christian, I am confident that the message of the Bible, that God so loves mankind, has a powerful impact on those who are truly seeking to live good lives that are loving towards both God and man. Any man or women of good will would not want to worship a God who is hateful.

Fundamentally, *The 9/11 Verses* are about hate. This hate is wrapped up in a disguise of dedication and service to Allah. The message of Christ, that God loves us and He wants us to love Him and our neighbors, is truly a winning and captivating alternative to *The 9/11 Verses*.

Optimism with realism

Although I am optimistic, I understand the threat that Islamic scriptures pose continues to be very real. The inflammatory content of *The 9/11 Verses* guarantees that in the coming years there will be more Islamic violence.

But I am confident that those who love freedom, will, like the generations before them, meet these challenges and, in the process, will survive, grow and prosper.

Appendix

The 9/11 Verses Revealed

From the Koran and Hadith

This appendix contains all the verses from the Koran and passages from the Hadith that were used in each chapter. They are classified primarily by each of the four major elements in Islam that cause Muslim violence. Here in one place are the hidden *9/11 Verses*.

Islam 101

Infidels now are they who say, "God is the Messiah, son of Mary;" for the Messiah said, "O children of Israel! Worship God, my Lord and your Lord." Whoever shall join other gods with Allah, Allah shall forbid him the Garden, and his abode shall be the Fire; and the wicked shall have no helpers. They surely are infidels who say, "God is the third of three:" for there is no God but one God: and if they refrain not from what they say, a grievous chastisement shall light on such of them as are infidels. **The Koran, Chapter 5:76-77**

Attitude of hate towards non-Muslims

Believers! wage war against such of the infidels as are your neighbors, and let them find you rigorous: and know that Allah is with those who fear him.

The Koran, Chapter 9:123

Muslim Hadith Book 19, number 4457

The Messenger of Allah (may peace be upon him) used not to kill the children, so thou shouldst not kill them unless ...you could distinguish between a child who would grow up to he a believer (and a child who would grow up to be a non-believer), so that you killed the (prospective) non-believer and left the (prospective) believer aside.

O believers! Take not infidels for friends rather than believers. Would you furnish Allah with clear right to punish you?
                                    The Koran, Chapter 4:143

They desire that ye should be infidels that ye should be alike. Take therefore none of them for friends, till they have fled their homes for the cause of Allah. If they turn back, then seize them, and slay them wherever ye find them...
                                    The Koran, Chapter 4:91

O believers! take not the Jews or Christians as friends. They are but one another's friends. If any one taketh them for his friends, he surely is one of them! Allah will not guide the evil doers.   **The Koran, Chapter 5:56**

O ye who believe! Take not My foe and your foe for friends, shewing them kindness, although they believe not the truth which hath come to you: they drive forth the apostles and yourselves because ye believe in Allah your Lord! If you go forth to fight on My way, and from a desire to please Me, and

Appendix

shew them kindness in private, I well know what you conceal, and what ye discover! Whoso doth this hath already gone astray from even the way.   The Koran, Chapter 60:1

Muhammad is the Apostle of Allah; and his comrades are vehement against the infidels, but full of tenderness among themselves.   The Koran, Chapter 48:8

...Verily, the infidels are your undoubted enemies!
The Koran, Chapter 4:102

Muslim Hadith Book 38, Number 4447
Narrated by Abdullah ibn Abbas

The Prophet (peace be upon him) said: If you find anyone doing as Lot's people did, kill the one who does it, and the one to whom it is done.

Muslim Hadith Book 38, Number 4469
Narrated by AbuHurayrah

The Prophet (peace be upon him) said: If he is intoxicated, flog him; again if he is intoxicated, flog him; again if he is intoxicated, flog him if he does it again a fourth time, kill him.

Muslim Hadith Book 019, Number 4366

It has been narrated by 'Umar b. al-Khattib that he heard the Messenger of Allah (may peace be upon him) say: I will expel the Jews and Christians from the Arabian Peninsula and will not leave any but Muslim.

The 9/11 Verses

Bukhari Hadith Volume 4, Book 52, Number 256
Narrated by As-Sab bin Jaththama

The Prophet passed by me at a place called Al-Abwa or Waddan, and was asked whether it was permissible to attack the pagan warriors at night with the probability of exposing their women and children to danger. The Prophet replied, "They (i.e. women and children) are from them (i.e. pagans)."

Muslim Hadith Book 037, Number 6665

Abu Musa' reported that Allah's Messenger (may peace be upon him) said: When it will be the Day of Resurrection Allah would deliver to every Muslim a Jew or a Christian and say: That is your rescue from Hell-Fire.

Muslim Hadith Book 037, Number 6666

Abu Burda reported on the authority of his father that Allah's Apostle (may peace be upon him) said: No Muslim would die but Allah would admit in his stead a Jew or a Christian in Hell-Fire.

Muslim Hadith Book 037, Number 6668

Abu Burda reported Allah's Messenger (may peace be upon him) as saying: There would come people amongst the Muslims on the Day of Resurrection with as heavy sins as a mountain, and Allah would forgive them and He would place in their stead the Jews and the Christians.

Commands to kill non-Muslims

Muslim Hadith Book 14, Number 2635
Narrated by Anas ibn Malik

The Prophet (peace be upon him) said: "I am commanded to fight with men till they testify that there is no god but Allah, and that Muhammad is His servant and His Apostle, face our qiblah (direction of prayer), eat what we slaughter, and pray like us. When they do that, their life and property are unlawful for us except what is due to them. They will have the same rights as the Muslims have, and have the same responsibilities as the Muslims have."

Muslim Hadith Book 019, Number 4436

It has been narrated on the authority of Jabir that the Messenger of Allah (may peace be upon him) said: Who will kill Ka'b b. Ashraf? He has maligned Allah, the Exalted, and His Messenger. Muhammad b. Maslama said: Messenger of Allah, do you wish that I should kill him? He said: Yes. He said: Permit me to talk (to him in the way I deem fit). He said: Talk (as you like).

So, Muhammad b. Maslama came to Ka'b and talked to him, referred to the old friendship between them and said: This man (i.e. the Holy Prophet) has made up his mind to collect charity (from us) and this has put us to a great hardship. When he heard this, Ka'b said: By God, you will be put to more trouble by him. Muhammad b. Maslama said: No doubt, now we have become his followers and we do not like to forsake him until we see what turn his affairs will take. I want that you should give me a loan.

He said: What will you mortgage? He said: What do you want? He said: Pledge me your women. He said: You are the most handsome of the Arabs; should we pledge our women to you? He said: Pledge me your children. He said: The son of one of us may abuse us saying that he was pledged for two wasqs (300 lbs.) of dates, but we can pledge you (cur) weapons. He said: All right.

Then Muhammad b. Maslama promised that he would come to him with Harith, Abu 'Abs b. Jabr and Abbad b. Bishr. So they came and called upon him at night. He came down to them. Sufyan says that all the narrators except 'Amr have stated that his wife said: I hear a voice which sounds like the voice of murder. He said: It is only Muhammad b. Maslama and his foster-brother, Abu Na'ila. When a gentleman is called at night even it to be pierced with a spear, he should respond to the call.

Muhammad said to his companions: As he comes down, I will extend my hands towards his head and when I hold him fast, you should do your job. So when he came down and he was holding his cloak under his arm, they said to him: We sense from you a very fine smell.

He said: Yes, I have with me a mistress who is the most scented of the women of Arabia. He said: Allow me to smell (the scent on your head). He said: Yes, you may smell. So he caught it and smelt. Then he said: Allow me to do so (once again).

He then held his head fast and said to his companions: Do your job. And they killed him.

Appendix

Muslim Hadith Book 38, Number 4348
Narrated by Abdullah Ibn Abbas

A blind man had a slave-mother who used to abuse the Prophet (peace be upon him) and disparage him. He forbade her but she did not stop. He rebuked her but she did not give up her habit. One night she began to slander the Prophet (peace be upon him) and abuse him.

So he took a dagger, placed it on her belly, pressed it, and killed her. A child who came between her legs was smeared with the blood that was there. When the morning came, the Prophet (peace be upon him) was informed about it.

He assembled the people and said: I adjure by Allah the man who has done this action and I adjure him by my right to him that he should stand up. Jumping over the necks of the people and trembling the man stood up.

He sat before the Prophet (peace be upon him) and said: Apostle of Allah! I am her master; she used to abuse you and disparage you. I forbade her, but she did not stop, and I rebuked her, but she did not abandon her habit. I have two sons like pearls from her, and she was my companion. Last night she began to abuse and disparage you. So I took a dagger, put it on her belly and pressed it till I killed her.

Thereupon the Prophet (peace be upon him) said: Oh be witness, no retaliation is payable for her blood.

Muslim Hadith Book 38, Number 4349
Narrated by Ali ibn AbuTalib

A Jewess used to abuse the Prophet (peace be upon him) and disparage him. A man strangled her till she died. The Apostle of Allah (peace be upon him) declared that no recompense was payable for her blood.

The 9/11 Verses

Muslim Hadith Book 38, Number 4421
Narrated by Al-Lajlaj al-Amiri

I was working in the market. A woman passed carrying a child. The people rushed towards her, and I also rushed along with them.

I then went to the Prophet (peace be upon him) while he was asking: Who is the father of this (child) who is with you? She remained silent.

A young man by her side said: I am his father, Apostle of Allah! He then turned towards her and asked: Who is the father of this child with you?

The young man said: I am his father, Apostle of Allah! The Apostle of Allah (peace be upon him) then looked at some of those who were around him and asked them about him. They said: We only know good (about him).

The Prophet (peace be upon him) said to him: Are you married? He said: Yes. So he gave orders regarding him and he was stoned to death.

He (the narrator) said: We took him out, dug a pit for him and put him in it. We then threw stones at him until he died.

Bakhari Hadith Volume 8, Book 82, Number 806
Narrated by Abu Huraira

A man came to Allah's Apostle while he was in the mosque, and he called him, saying, "O Allah's Apostle! I have committed illegal sexual intercourse." The Prophet turned his face to the other side, but that man repeated his statement four times, and after he bore witness against himself four times, the Prophet called him, saying, "Are you mad?" The man said, "No." The Prophet said, "Are you married?" The man said, "Yes." Then the Prophet said, "Take him away and stone him to death." Jabir bin 'Abdullah said: I was among the ones who participated in stoning him and we stoned him at the Musalla. When the stones troubled him, he fled, but we over took him at Al-Harra and stoned him to death.

Bakhari Hadith Volume 8, Book 82, Number 809
Narrated by Ibn 'Umar

A Jew and a Jewess were brought to Allah's Apostle on a charge of committing an illegal sexual intercourse. The Prophet asked them. "What is the legal punishment (for this sin) in your Book (Torah)?"

They replied, "Our priests have innovated the punishment of blackening the faces with charcoal and Tajbiya." 'Abdullah bin Salam said, "O Allah's Apostle, tell them to bring the Torah." The Torah was brought, and then one of the Jews put his hand over the Divine Verse of the Rajam (stoning to death) and started reading what preceded and what followed it.

On that, Ibn Salam said to the Jew, "Lift up your hand." Behold! The Divine Verse of the Rajam was under his hand. So Allah's Apostle ordered that the two (sinners) be stoned to death, and so they were stoned. Ibn 'Umar added: So both of them were stoned at the Balat and I saw the Jew sheltering the Jewess.

Muslim Hadith Book 017, Number 4207

Imran b. Husain reported that a woman from Juhaina came to Allah's Apostle (may peace be upon him) and she had become pregnant because of adultery. She said: Allah's Apostle, I have done something for which (prescribed punishment) must be imposed upon me, so impose that. Allah's Apostle (may peace be upon him) called her master and said: Treat her well, and when she delivers bring her to me. He did accordingly.

Then Allah's Apostle (may peace be upon him) pronounced judgment about her and her clothes were tied around her and then he commanded and she was stoned to death. He then prayed over her (dead body). Thereupon Umar said to him: Allah's Apostle, you offer prayer for her, whereas she had committed adultery!

Thereupon he said: She has made such a repentance that if it were to be divided among seventy men of Medina, it would be enough. Have you found any repentance better than this that she sacrificed her life for Allah, the Majestic?

Muslim Hadith Book 14, Number 2632
Narrated by Salamah ibn al-Akwa'

The Apostle of Allah (peace be upon him) appointed AbuBakr our commander and we fought with some people who were polytheists, and we attacked them at night, killing them. Our war cry that night was "put to death; put to death." Salamah said: I killed that night with my hand polytheists belonging to seven houses.

Muslim Hadith Book 14, Number 2664
Narrated by Samurah ibn Jundub

The Prophet (peace be upon him) said: Kill the old men who are polytheists, but spare their children.

"Fight then against them (non-Muslims) till strife be at an end, and the religion be all of it Allah's."

The Koran, Chapter 8:40

Appendix

Make war upon such of those to whom the Scriptures have been given as believe not in Allah, or in the Last Day, and who forbid not that which Allah and His Apostle have forbidden, and who profess not the profession of truth, until they pay tribute out of hand, and they be humbled.

The Koran, Chapter 9:29

Believers! wage war against such of the infidels as are your neighbors, and let them find you rigorous: and know that Allah is with those who fear him.

The Koran, Chapter 9:123

O Prophet! Make war on the infidels and hypocrites, and deal rigorously with them. **The Koran, Chapter 66:9**

Bukhari Hadith Volume 4, Book 52, Number 50
Narrated by Anas bin Malik

The Prophet said, "A single endeavor (of fighting) in Allah's Cause in the forenoon or in the afternoon is better than the world and whatever is in it."

Bukhari Hadith Volume 4, Book 52, Number 176
Narrated by 'Abdullah bin 'Umar

Allah's Apostle said, "You (i.e. Muslims) will fight with the Jews till some of them will hide behind stones. The stones will (betray them) saying, 'O 'Abdullah (i.e. slave of Allah)! There is a Jew hiding behind me; so kill him.'"

The 9/11 Verses

Bukhari Hadith Volume 8, Book 82, Number 795
Narrated by Anas

The Prophet cut off the hands and feet of the men belonging to the tribe of 'Uraina and did not cauterize (their bleeding limbs) till they died.

Bukhari Hadith Volume 9, Book 84, Number 64
Narrated by 'Ali

No doubt I heard Allah's Apostle saying, "During the last days there will appear some young foolish people who will say the best words but their faith will not go beyond their throats (i.e. they will have no faith) and will go out from (leave) their religion as an arrow goes out of the game. So, where-ever you find them, kill them, for who-ever kills them shall have reward on the Day of Resurrection."

When ye encounter the infidels, strike off their heads till ye have made a great slaughter among them, and of the rest make fast the fetters. And afterwards let their either be free dismissals or ransomings, till the war hath laid down its burdens. Thus do. Were such the pleasure of Allah, He could Himself take vengeance upon them: but He would rather prove the one of you by the other.

And whoso fight for the cause of Allah, their words He will not suffer to miscarry; He will vouchsafe them guidance, and dispose their hearts aright; And He will bring them into Paradise, of which He hath told them. Believers! if ye help Allah, Allah will help you, and will set your feet firm: But as for the infidels, let them perish: and their works shall Allah bring to nought. The Koran, Chapter 47:4-9

Commands to force Islamic beliefs on non-Muslims

Muslim Hadith Book 019, Number 4363

It has been narrated on the authority of Abu Huraira who said: We were (sitting) in the mosque when the Messenger of Allah (may peace be upon him) came to us and said: (Let us) go to the Jews. We went out with him until we came to them. The Messenger of Allah (may peace be upon him) stood up and called out to them (saying): O ye assembly of Jews, accept Islam (and) you will be safe.

They said: Abu'l-Qasim, you have communicated (God's Message to us). The Messenger of Allah (may peace be upon him) said: I want this (i.e. you should admit that God's Message has been communicated to you), accept Islam and you would be safe.

They said: Abu'l-Qisim, you have communicated (Allah's Message). The Messenger of Allah (may peace be upon him) said: I want this... He said to them (the same words) the third time (and on getting the same reply) he added: You should know that the earth belongs to Allah and His Apostle, and I wish that I should expel you from this land. Those of you who have any property with them should sell it, otherwise they should know that the earth belongs to Allah and His Apostle (and they may have to go away leaving everything behind).

Muslim Hadith Book 019, Number 4364

It has been narrated on the authority of Ibn Umar that the Jews of Banu Nadir and Banu Quraizi fought against the Messenger of Allah (may peace be upon him) who expelled Banu Nadir, and allowed Quraiza to stay on, and granted favour to them until they too fought against him. Then he killed their men, and distributed their women, children and properties among the Muslims, except that some of them had joined the Messenger of Allah (may peace be upon him) who granted them security. They embraced Islam.

The Messenger of Allah (may peace be upon him) turned out all the Jews of Medina. Banu Qainuqa' (the tribe of 'Abdullah b. Salim) and the Jews of Banu Haritha and every other Jew who was in Medina.

Bukhari Hadith Volume 4, Book 52, Number 196
Narrated by Abu Huraira

Allah's Apostle said, "I have been ordered to fight with the people till they say, 'None has the right to be worshiped but Allah,' and whoever says, 'None has the right to be worshiped but Allah,' his life and property will be saved by me except for Islamic law, and his accounts will be with Allah, (either to punish him or to forgive him.)"

...kill those who join other gods with Allah (polytheist Arabs) wherever ye shall find them; and seize them; besiege them, and lay wait for them with every kind of ambush: but if they shall convert, and observe prayer, and pay the obligatory alms, then let them go their way, for Allah is gracious, merciful.

The Koran, Chapter 9:4

When the help of Allah and the victory arrive, and thou seest men entering the religion of Allah by troops; Then utter the praise of thy Lord...   **The Koran, Chapter 110:1**

Appendix

Muslim Hadith Book 019, Number 4294

It has been reported from Sulaiman b. Buraid through his father that when the Messenger of Allah (may peace be upon him) appointed anyone as leader of an army or detachment he would especially exhort him to fear Allah and to be good to the Muslims who were with him.

He would say: Fight in the name of Allah and in the way of Allah. Fight against those who disbelieve in Allah. Make a holy war, do not embezzle the spoils; do not break your pledge; and do not mutilate (the dead) bodies; do not kill the children.

When you meet your enemies who are polytheists, invite them to three courses of action. If they respond to any one of these, you also accept it and withhold yourself from doing them any harm. Invite them to (accept) Islam; if they respond to you, accept it from them and desist from fighting against them. Then invite them to migrate from their lands to the land of Muhairs and inform them that, if they do so, they shall have all the privileges and obligations of the Muhajirs.

If they refuse to migrate, tell them that they will have the status of Bedouin Muslims and will be subjected to the Commands of Allah like other Muslims, but they will not get any share from the spoils of war or Fai' except when they actually fight with the Muslims (against the disbelievers).

If they refuse to accept Islam, demand from them the Jizya. If they agree to pay, accept it from them and hold off your hands. If they refuse to pay the tax, seek Allah's help and fight them.

When you lay siege to a fort and the besieged appeal to you for protection in the name of Allah and His Prophet, do not accord to them the guarantee of Allah and His Prophet, but accord to them your own guarantee and the guarantee of your companions for it is a lesser sin that the security given by you or your companions be disregarded than that the security granted in the name of Allah and His Prophet be violated.

When you besiege a fort and the besieged want you to let them out in accordance with Allah's Command, do not let them come out in accordance with His Command, but do so at your (own) command, for you do not know whether or not you will be able to carry out Allah's behest with regard to them.

Bukhari Hadith Volume 4, Book 52, Number 260
Narrated by Ikrima

Ali burnt some people and this news reached Ibn 'Abbas, who said, "Had I been in his place I would not have burnt them, as the Prophet said, 'Don't punish (anybody) with Allah's Punishment.' No doubt, I would have killed them, for the Prophet said, 'If somebody (a Muslim) discards his religion, kill him.'"

Bukhari Hadith Volume 9, Book 83, Number 37
Narrated by Abu Qilaba

By Allah, Allah's Apostle never killed anyone except in one of the following three situations: (1) A person who killed somebody unjustly, was killed (in Qisas,) (2) a married person who committed illegal sexual intercourse and (3) a man who fought against Allah and His Apostle and deserted Islam and became an apostate.

Bukhari Hadith Volume 9, Book 89, Number 271
Narrated by Abu Musa

A man embraced Islam and then reverted back to Judaism. Mu'adh bin Jabal came and saw the man with Abu Musa. Mu'adh asked, "What is wrong with this (man)?" Abu Musa replied, "He embraced Islam and then reverted back to Judaism." Mu'adh said, "I will not sit down unless you kill him (as it is) the verdict of Allah and His Apostle."

Promised reward of Heaven for violence against non-Muslims

Muslim Hadith Book 14, Number 2507
Narrated by Uqbah ibn Amir

I heard the Apostle of Allah (peace be upon him) say: Allah, Most High, will cause three persons to enter Paradise for one arrow: the maker when he has a good motive in making it, the one who shoots it, and the one who hands it; so shoot and ride, but your shooting is dearer to me than your riding.

Muslim Hadith Book 14, Number 2520
Narrated by Abdullah ibn Amr ibn al-'As

The Prophet (peace be upon him) said: The warrior gets his reward, and the one who equips him gets his own reward and that of the warrior.

But, for the Allah-fearing is a blissful abode, enclosed gardens and vineyards; and damsels with swelling breasts, peers in age...   The Koran, Chapter 78:31

And theirs shall be the Houris, with large dark eyes, like pearls hidden in their shells...   The Koran, Chapter 56:22

But the pious shall be in a secure place, amid gardens and foun-tains, clothed in silk and richest robes, facing one another. Thus it shall be: and We will wed them to the virgins with large dark eyes. The Koran, Chapter 44:51-54

Al-Tirmidhi Hadith 2687

Mohammad said: The least reward for the people of paradise is 80,000 servants and 72 wives.

Al-Tirmidhi Hadith 5636
Narrated by Anas ibn Malik

The Prophet (peace be upon him) said, "In Paradise, the believer will be given such and such power to conduct sexual intercourse." He was asked whether he would be capable of that and replied that he would be given the capacity of a hundred men.

Muslim Hadith Book 14, Number 2515
Narrated by Hasana' daughter of Mu'awiyah

She reported on the authority of her paternal uncle: I asked the Prophet (peace be upon him): Who are in Paradise? He replied: Prophets are in Paradise, martyrs are in Paradise, infants are in Paradise and children buried alive are in Paradise.

Muslim Hadith Book 14, Number 2535
Narrated by Mu'adh ibn Jabal

The Apostle of Allah (peace be upon him) said: If anyone fights in Allah's path as long as the time between two milkings of a she-camel, Paradise will be assured for him. If anyone sincerely asks Allah for being killed and then dies or is killed, there will be a reward of a martyr for him.

Ibn al-Musaffa added from here: If anyone is wounded in Allah's path, or suffers a misfortune, it will come on the Day of Resurrection as copious as possible, its color saffron, and its odor musk; and if anyone suffers from ulcers while in Allah's path, he will have on him the stamp of the martyrs.

Verily, of the faithful hath Allah bought their persons and their substance, on condition of Paradise for them in return: on the path of Allah shall they fight, and slay, and be slain...Rejoice, therefore in the contract that ye have contracted: for this shall be a great bliss.

The Koran, Chapter 9:112

Bukhari Hadith Volume 4, Book 52, Number 46
Narrated by Abu Huraira

I heard Allah's Apostle saying, "The example of a Mujahid in Allah's Cause — and Allah knows better who really strives in His Cause — is like a person who fasts and prays continuously. Allah guarantees that He will admit the Mujahid in His Cause into Paradise if he is killed, otherwise He will return him to his home safely with rewards and war booty."

Bukhari Hadith Volume 4, Book 52, Number 73
Narrated by 'Abdullah bin Abi Aufa

Allah's Apostle said, "Know that Paradise is under the shades of swords."

The 9/11 Verses

Bukhari Hadith Volume 4, Book 52, Number 44
Narrated by Abu Huraira

A man came to Allah's Apostle and said, "Instruct me as to such a deed as equals Jihad in reward." He replied, "I do not find such a deed."

Bukhari Hadith Volume 4, Book 52, Number 50
Narrated by Anas bin Malik

The Prophet said, "A single endeavor (of fighting) in Allah's Cause in the forenoon or in the afternoon is better than the world and whatever is in it."

Bukhari Hadith Volume 4, Book 52, Number 63
Narrated by Al-Bara

A man whose face was covered with an iron mask (i.e. clad in armor) came to the Prophet and said, "O Allah's Apostle! Shall I fight or embrace Islam first?" The Prophet said, "Embrace Islam first and then fight." So he embraced Islam, and was martyred. Allah's Apostle said, A little work, but a great reward. "(He did very little (after embracing Islam), but he will be rewarded in abundance)."

Bukhari Hadith Volume 4, Book 52, Number 53
Narrated by Anas bin Malik

The Prophet said, "Nobody who dies and finds good from Allah (in the Hereafter) would wish to come back to this world even if he were given the whole world and whatever is in it, except the martyr who, on seeing the superiority of martyrdom, would like to come back to the world and get killed again (in Allah's Cause)."

Appendix

Bukhari Hadith Volume 4, Book 52, Number 64
Narrated by Anas bin Malik

Um Ar-Rubai'bint Al-Bara', the mother of Hartha bin Suraqa came to the Prophet and said, "O Allah's Prophet! Will you tell me about Hartha?" Hartha has been killed (i.e. martyred) on the day of Badr with an arrow thrown by an unidentified person. She added, "If he is in Paradise, I will be patient; otherwise, I will weep bitterly for him." He said, "O mother of Hartha! There are Gardens in Paradise and your son got the Firdausal-ala (i.e. the best place in Paradise)."

Bukhari Hadith Volume 4, Book 52, Number 72
Narrated by Anas bin Malik

The Prophet said, "Nobody who enters Paradise likes to go back to the world even if he got everything on the earth, except a Mujahid who wishes to return to the world so that he may be martyred ten times because of the dignity he receives (from Allah)."

Narrated by Al-Mughira bin Shu'ba:

Our Prophet told us about the message of our Lord that "Whoever amongst us is killed will go to Paradise." Umar asked the Prophet, "Is it not true that our men who are killed will go to Paradise and theirs (i.e. those of the Pagan's) will go to the (Hell) fire?" The Prophet said, "Yes."

Bukhari Hadith Volume 4, Book 52, Number 175
Narrated by Khalid bin Madan

That 'Umair bin Al-Aswad Al-Anasi told him that he went to 'Ubada bin As-Samit while he was staying in his house at the sea-shore of Hims with (his wife) Um Haram. 'Umair said. Um Haram informed us that she heard the Prophet saying,

"Paradise is granted to the first batch of my followers who will undertake a naval expedition." Um Haram added, "I said, 'O Allah's Apostle! Will I be amongst them?' He replied, 'You are amongst them.' The Prophet then said, 'The first army amongst my followers who will invade Caesar's City will be forgiven their sins.' I asked, 'Will I be one of them, O Allah's Apostle?' He replied in the negative."

Muslim Hadith Book 14, Number 2516
Narrated by AbudDarda'

The Prophet (peace be upon him) said: The intercession of a martyr will be accepted for seventy members of his family.

Muslim Hadith Book 14, Number 2482
Narrated by Thabit ibn Qays

A woman called Umm Khallad came to the Prophet (peace be upon him) while she was veiled. She was searching for her son who had been killed (in the battle). Some of the Companions of the Prophet (peace be upon him) said to her: You have come here asking for your son while veiling your face? She said: If I am afflicted with the loss of my son, I shall not suffer the loss of my modesty. The Apostle of Allah (peace be upon him) said: You will get the reward of two martyrs for your son. She asked: Why is that so, Apostle of Allah? He replied: Because the people of the Book have killed him.

Muslim Hadith Book 14, Number 2497
Narrated by AbuUmamah

The Prophet (peace be upon him) said: He who does not join the warlike expedition (jihad), or equip, or looks well after a warrior's family when he is away, will be smitten by Allah

196

with a sudden calamity. *Yazid ibn Abdu Rabbihi said in his tradition: "before the Day of Resurrection."*

Muslim Hadith Book 019, Number 4413

It has been reported on the authority of Anas b. Malik that (when the enemy got the upper hand) on the day of the Battle of Uhud, the Messenger of Allah (may peace be upon him) was left with only seven men from the ansar and two men from the Quraish. When the enemy advanced towards him and overwhelmed him, he said:

Whoso turns them away from us will attain Paradise or will be my Companion in Paradise.

A man from the Ansar came forward and fought (the enemy) until he was killed. The enemy advanced and over-whelmed him again and he repeated the words: Whoso turns them away, from us will attain Paradise or will be my Companion in Paradise.

A man from the Ansar came forward and fought until he was killed. This state continued until the seven Ansar were killed (one after the other). Now, the Messenger of Allah (may peace be upon him) said to his two Companions: We have not done justice to our Companions.

Commands that support slavery

Happy now the believers... who restrain their appetites, (save with their wives, or the slaves whom their right hands possess): for in that case they shall be free from blame...

The Koran, Chapter 23:1-5

Bukhari Hadith Volume 5, Book 59, Number 459
Narrated by Ibn Muhairiz

I entered the Mosque and saw Abu Said Al-Khudri and sat beside him and asked him about Al-Azl (i.e. coitus interruptus). Abu Said said, "We went out with Allah's Apostle for the Ghazwa of Banu Al-Mustaliq and we received captives from among the Arab captives and we desired women and celibacy became hard on us and we loved to do coitus interruptus. So when we intended to do coitus interruptus, we said, 'How can we do coitus interruptus before asking Allah's Apostle who is present among us?' We asked (him) about it and he said, 'It is better for you not to do so, for if any soul (till the Day of Resurrection) is predestined to exist, it will exist.' "

Commands instituting temporary marriage

Bukhari Hadith Volume 6, Book 60, Number 139
Narrated by Abdullah Ibn Abbas

We used to participate in the holy wars carried on by the Prophet and we had no women (wives) with us. So we said (to the Prophet). "Shall we castrate ourselves?" But the Prophet forbade us to do that and thenceforth he allowed us to marry a woman (temporarily) by giving her even a garment, and then he recited: "O you who believe! Do not make unlawful the good things which Allah has made lawful for you."

Index

Index

About the Author

Karl J. Trautwein became interested in the connection between the Koran and terrorism as a result of the 9/11 Islamic terrorist attacks. After years of following the issue via the mainstream media, he decided the information he was receiving was incomplete and confusing. So in 2006, he decided to find out the truth for himself.

The author has spent over two years studying the Islamic faith. His approach was to personally read the Koran and pertinent portions of the Hadith (the sayings and deeds of Muhammad). In addition, he reviewed writings by those who teach, interpret and comment on the Koran and Hadith.

From his research, Karl has discovered the true connection between the Koran and terrorism. He has distilled these Islamic terrorist teachings for presentation in this book and has called them *The 9/11 Verses*.

The author holds undergraduate and masters degrees in finance and business management. In the corporate world, he has been a chief financial officer, chief operating officer and member of the board of directors of manufacturing and construction firms. Karl currently divides his time between managing his real estate investment companies and writing.

The 9/11 Verses by **Karl J. Trautwein** is available through your favorite book dealer or the publisher:

Now I See! Publishing
Box 352
Etiwanda, CA 91739
Phone: 909-922-7276
Website: www.The911Verses.com

The 9/11 Verses **(ISBN: 978-0-9820273-0-1)** is $24.95 for hardbound edition, plus $5.50 shipping for first copy ($2.00 each additional copy) and sales tax for CA orders.